THE LEGEND OF ZOLA MAHOBE

and the **Mamelodi Sundowns** Story

DON LEPATI
and **NIKOLAOS KIRKINIS**

TAFELBERG

Tafelberg
An imprint of NB Publishers
A division of Media24 Boeke (Pty) Ltd
40 Heerengracht, Cape Town, 8000
www.tafelberg.com

© 2022 Don Lepati

All rights reserved
No part of this book may be reproduced or transmitted in any form
or by any electronic or mechanical means, including photocopying
and recording, or by any other information storage or retrieval system,
without written permission from the publisher.

Cover design by Wilna Combrinck
Book design by Marthie Steenkamp
Edited by Russel Brownlee
Proofread by Sally Hofmeyr

Note about the cover image:
Despite an extensive search, NB has not been able to trace rights-
holder to this photograph. If the copyright holder gets in touch with us,
we will rectify the copyright information in any future editions.

Set in Tex Gyre Pagella
First edition, first impression 2022

ISBN: 978-0-624-09371-8
Epub: 978-0-624-09372-5

Printed by novus print, a division of Novus Holdings

Table of contents

Preface	7
The legend is born – *Kudela owaziyo*	9
In Soweto – *Ubaba uhambile ne side-chick*	17
Snowy Moshoeshoe – *Indoni yamanzi*	25
Studying the system – *Uvukile wazenzela*	30
Playing politics – *Uboshiwe eJohnVorster*	37
Mr Cool, Mr Big Bucks – *Imali eningi*	42
The early days of Mamelodi Sundowns – *Umlando*	54
Money can't buy loyalty – *Sofa silahlane*	83
Mother of all parties – *Ngisho abelungu abakhoni*	87
The betrayal – *Iphutha elikhulu*	103
The end of the game – *Sisenkingeni*	109
Snowy's trial – *Kuqulwa izesekeli*	117
Standard Bank takes over Sundowns – *Iphuciwe*	121
Mahobe's arrest – *Iqhawe elingumkhwabanisi*	124
The trial – *Viva Zola*	127
The Tsichlases and the Krok brothers – *Kuphethe abasha*	135
The bid to get 'Mr Cool' out – *Makadedelwe!*	141
In Barberton Prison – *Is'boshwa siphenduka i-Is!am*	150

Release from prison – *Indodana yolahleko*	163
Motsepe takes over Sundowns – *Iphupho le Africa*	170
The curtain falls – *Kwacisha ukukhanya*	173
Mauser, Mr Cool – *Dloz'lam*	177
A tribute by Natasha Tsichlas	182
Characters in the book and past players	184
Acknowledgements	190
About the author	192

Preface

There are many legends of South African club soccer, but none more legendary than Zola Mahobe, the father of present-day Mamelodi Sundowns. When Mahobe burst onto the soccer scene I was a twenty-something living in Lesotho. Sundowns was a fashionable team and I used to goggle at Mahobe for his free-spending approach when it came to buying players and the way he thrust not only the club but also himself into the spotlight. He seemed to have a wallet that never stopped giving. I also loved the style of soccer that Mamelodi Sundowns played, fondly referred to as the 'shoeshine and piano' style by their flamboyant coach, Screamer Tshabalala.

Then Mahobe's girlfriend, Snowy Moshoeshoe, got arrested. Mahobe was nowhere to be found and became a wanted man. The story doing the rounds in Lesotho was that Snowy, who worked at Standard Bank, had been taking one cent per day from all Standard Bank's clients and crediting Mahobe's bank account with the money, which amounted to millions of rands. But this was not how it happened.

Years later I relocated from Lesotho to South Africa, and I still followed Sundowns and wanted to be part of its supporter mobilisation team. I came close when club co-owner Anastasia

(Natasha) Tsichlas agreed that I could join the team on a trial basis. But for unforeseen reasons, this did not happen.

But my yearning for close family ties with Sundowns would not leave me. In 2016, by happy coincidence, I found myself in the company of a close acquaintance and we started to talk about my aspirations as a writer. Then our conversation drifted and we started to talk about Mahobe, who had died a few years earlier. He persuaded me to write a book about him.

I fell in love with the idea. But I did not want to delve into his private life beyond a certain point. What I wanted to do was to tell a story that would be enjoyed by soccer fans and those who love stories of intrigue – an entertaining account of his highs and lows. I wanted to 'collect' his spirit and bring it home where it belongs: in the hearts and minds of Mamelodi Sundowns supporters, soccer fans, and ordinary South Africans.

It was also important to paint the setting of the story – from Sophiatown to Soweto, from the politics of apartheid to the emergence of Black Power, from the role of sports boycott against South Africa to the significance of soccer in the fight against apartheid, and from the beginnings of Sundowns to present-day Mamelodi Sundowns.

This book is therefore not a detailed account of Mahobe's life, but one of his journey with Mamelodi Sundowns and his influence on South African soccer. It is also a portrait of a larger-than-life Sowetan who, from humble beginnings, turned himself into a jet-setting multimillionaire by continuously robbing a bank and splashing his loot in full view of everyone.

The legend is born
– *Kudela owaziyo*

It was New Year's Day, 1954, and it was starting to rain again in Sophiatown, an overpopulated shantytown just outside Johannesburg. It had been raining on and off since first light; a soft patter on the roof, and then a torrent of bigger drops blocking conversations for those already-numb ears.

It had been raining on and off since Monday and it was only on Thursday, New Year's Eve, that the skies began to open up. The streets became abuzz with people escaping their crowded, stuffy corrugated metal shanties to breathe the fresh air in the sun. That evening, the newlywed Mahobes and their friends went out to the Odin to celebrate New Year's Eve. The Odin was an upmarket movie hall and was the pride of Sophiatown. It sat 1 200 people and was the largest theatre in South Africa. It also hosted dance parties and stage performances and was known to host multiracial acts that played to multiracial audiences.

Speakers were placed outside, and the hall was buzzing with revellers, both inside and outside. The Mahobes and their friends sat outside, making merry to the sounds of jazz and the festive atmosphere. The young Mrs Mahobe, heavy with child, sat on a sofa that they had borrowed from a neighbour. She dared not risk dancing lest the baby decide to misbehave. She was due any time now. She just sat there, taking in the atmosphere and whispering a lullaby.

As the clock hit midnight, the music took on a higher tempo and there were shouts of *'Happeee!'* everywhere. Then the band played *Nkosi Sikelel' iAfrika*, and everyone inside and outside the hall joined in the chorus. It was a new year, another year of struggle. But the people had hope that God would indeed bless South Africa and that one day, not far into the future, things would get better.

It was around two in the morning when the young Mrs Mahobe decided it was time they left for home. 'Love, I feel tired; I think we should go home,' she said to her husband.

'Ok, my love; ten more minutes. I must arrange for someone to take the sofa back.'

The clouds had started to gather and there were flashes of lightning far away on the horizon. The rain was threatening again. It would not be long now.

It started to pour only a few hours after they arrived back at their shack, which they shared with another couple. The rain caused havoc in the streets as revellers scrambled for cover while others, overcome by intoxication, continued to dance in the rain. But something else was happening. The young Mrs Mahobe was beginning to have contractions. Like outside, with the rain pouring down and making people run for cover, the room erupted into a hive of activity of its own. There was the first contraction, followed by another only a few minutes later. They had thought that they would get an earlier warning that the baby was due: contractions coming at long intervals and then quickening over a longer period, giving them plenty of time to prepare.

The rumble of thunder rattled the windowpanes as the young Mr Mahobe paced the room from one end to the other, trying to find something – some instrument, some medicine, some divine intervention that could take the pain away from his wife.

'Try to stay calm!' shouted someone over the deafening noise of the rain. 'Somebody get me some warm water and a towel!'

Outside, the music continued to pierce the air amid sporadic shouts of *'Happeee!'*

'Why are they taking so long?' said the panic-stricken nurse who had been summoned to the Mahobes' shack. She knew it would not be long now before the baby was born.

The ambulance arrived amid a wild frenzy in the Mahobes' shack. The baby was coming out. It was a baby boy.

It had stopped raining and the sun was beginning to break through the clouds when the ambulance left the crowded shack with mother, father and baby safe inside. There was a soothing calmness in the air now, and soft smiles of contentment on their faces. The newborn had stopped crying and was beginning to doze off. He was to be known as Zola Daniel Mahobe.

※ ※ ※

Such was life in Sophiatown, also fondly known as Sof'town or Kofifi by its swanky residents. The late Ntatemoholo Phahlane, a famous Sophiatown journalist, claimed to be the one who gave Sophiatown the nickname Kofifi, meaning a colourful and cosmopolitan little Black town.

Sophiatown was the centre of urban African music and culture, known for its bohemian lifestyle and peppy music scene. It was the home of kwela – the pennywhistle-based street music – and Marabi jazz; and its shebeens, speakeasies, and all-night dance parties were legendary. Shebeens and speakeasies were illegal watering holes where musicians, writers, artists, politicians, educators, intellectuals, gangsters, and workers would converge to socialise. Popular shebeens included the Church, so called because it was next to Christ the King Church; the Thirty-Nine Steps, which ironically had not a single step at the entrance; and the well-known Back of the Moon.

This was the home of famous ladies of jazz, such as the glamorous Dolly Rathebe, who was known for her sensual stage presence. She performed trademark African jazz tunes and African versions of American jazz favourites. There was also the great Dorothy Masuka, whose style consisted of African jive and swing jazz, and Mirriam Makeba, who first became noticed when she was with the Manhattan Brothers. The men of jazz included Jonas Gwangwa, Hugh Masekela, Early Mabuza and the legendary Kippie Moeketsi. According to Kippie, they would play nonstop from eight in the evening till four in the morning, and sometimes the tsotsis (young township criminals) would force them to play until the sun came up.

Sophiatown's culture was also influenced by the Picture Palace movie hall, also known as Balansky's, after its owner. Balansky's was second-rate compared to the Odin. Here, Sophiatown residents, especially the tsotsis, could watch popular American gangster movies of the time. Many township dwellers began to speak American slang, using phrases like 'Hey, Nigger', 'jeepers creepers', and 'cute chick'. Some even referred to certain parts of

Sophiatown as Little Harlem. The most popular movie was *The Street with No Name*, a gangster movie starring Richard Widmark, who played the character Alec Stiles (pronounced 'Styles' by the tsotsis). The hall would be filled to capacity by the tsotsis when it played. Widmark was the mob boss in the movie, and each time he appeared on screen the crowd would scream, 'Styles! Go it, Styles!' He wore a long overcoat, while his henchmen wore belted raincoats with slits at the back. So popular were American gangster movies that Sophiatown gangsters adopted their style and language, and expressions like 'Remember guys, I'm de brains of dis outfit!' became popular.

Sophiatown was also dubbed the 'Chicago' of South Africa because of its notorious gangs, such as the Berliners, Ma-Rashea, and the Americans. The Berliners used to wreak havoc on the areas under their control, killing, raping, and robbing the locals of whatever they had. They were alleged to have owned more guns than the local police station. The Ma-Rashea wore Basotho blankets over their smart city pants, completing the dress style with shiny shoes and smart hats decorated with an ostrich feather. They hated tsotsis like the Berliners and had a reputation for being ruthless when punishing them.

The Americans, on the other hand, did not prey on the Sophiatown community, but specialised in stealing goods from shops in the city and from railway delivery trucks. They were known to many as the African Robin Hoods because they stole goods from the rich Whites and sold them to the locals at give-away prices. Stealing from the Whites was not seen as a crime during those days, but as heroism – a form of political activism. It was taking back what had been taken away from the people by the apartheid regime. The Americans dressed in flashy 'American' clothes, drove fancy American-made cars, and loved girls. Their motto was: 'Live fast, die young, and leave a good-looking corpse'.

There were many other gangs in Sophiatown. Life was difficult under those conditions, and since most of the formally employed men worked at the mines, youngsters were unsupervised and could do whatever they liked. Many grew up to be gangsters. It was even tougher for women, many of whom worked as shebeen queens or assistants, or sold themselves on street corners as prostitutes.

Sophiatown was originally a farm outside Johannesburg, bought by a certain Hermann Tobiansky, who named it after his wife, Sophia. Subsequently, the area became a Whites-only area. But when the Johannesburg City Council built a sewage dump next to it, White people did not want to live there any more, and they moved away. Later, Tobiansky gave permission to Blacks and Coloureds to settle there. It was the one area in Johannesburg where Blacks were not required to have residence permits, as they were in other areas such as Soweto. Because of huge mortgage bonds and poverty, Black landowners allowed others to build shacks made of metal sheets in their backyards, and the population grew exponentially. The yards would have a single tap or no tap at all, and ablution facilities were a big problem. Sophiatown became a health hazard.

With the growth of Johannesburg, Sophiatown became encircled by White suburbs. The Whites did not want Blacks there. In June 1953, the slum clearance plans were announced, which targeted the removal of, among others, Sophiatown residents. In 1954, the Native Resettlement Board, which was responsible for drawing up and implementing operational plans for the removal and resettlement of Sophiatown residents in various parts of Soweto, served the first notices to residents informing them of its intention to resettle them.

In the early hours of 9 February 1955, around two thousand policemen armed with guns, knobkerries and rifles forcefully moved the families of Sophiatown to Meadowlands, Soweto.

Even though politicians tried to use the forced removals for politicking, and urged people to resist, many were happy to go, and they sang: 'Out to the Meadowlands we go, walking in the sunlight ...'. The houses were better in Meadowlands than in the slum that Sophiatown had become. There was no resistance, no demonstration, no disruption; just slogans remaining behind on the walls saying: 'Ons dak nie ... Ons phola hierso' ('We are not moving ... We are staying here').

There were those who stood to lose and those who stood to gain from the forced removals. The landlords, most of whom depended on the rentals they received from the backyard dwellers for their income, and the gangsters, who thrived in the ineffectively policed Sophiatown, stood to lose. These groups were vocal in resisting the removals. The poor, on the other hand, had more to gain by relocating to the 'roomy' Meadowlands houses.

Sophiatown was then torn down, and a new White suburb was built on its ruins. It was named Triomf, meaning 'triumph'. But that triumph did not last forever, and the suburb reverted to its original name in 2006.

Crime followed the people to Soweto. Criminals were called *botsotsi*. There were the hoodlum types who controlled the darkness and terrorised, robbed, and raped the locals, competing for girls and territory. There were the spivs and scallywags who conned and stole from unsuspecting locals and impressed girls with their stylish clothes. There were the Robin Hood types who stole from the Whites in the city and sold the items at give-away prices in the townships. And then there were the 'Big Boss' types who stole enough from the Whites to live the good life and establish their own businesses. It was the latter who would influence Mahobe's later life.

In Soweto

– Ubaba uhambile ne side-chick

Not long after the Mahobes moved to Meadowlands, Mr Mahobe left his family and went to live with his new lover. His mother soon followed suit: she also found herself another man and decided to move in with him. Mahobe's uncle, Harrison Selulu, who lived in one of the new township houses in Meadowlands, offered to raise him and took him in. Uncle Selulu was not married and had no children. He lived with his mother, Mahobe's grandmother; there were only the two of them in the house.

It was no big deal being raised by Uncle Selulu and his mother. Besides, it was not uncommon during those days for children to be separated from their parents. There was a wave of crime by township dwellers, and there was mass resistance against the injustices of the apartheid government. Young men and women were at the centre of it all and were often arrested or even killed. Some of the young men and women made babies and simply left them with their parents, uncles, or aunties to raise them.

They were not well off, Uncle Selulu and his mother, and they did not have much of a clue about how to nurture a boy who had been separated from his parents. Uncle Selulu's mother was old and rusty when it came to such duties, and Uncle Selulu had never raised a child. They did the best they could, but there was a void in Mahobe that only a parent could fill. He learned what he could from them, and the rest he learned from the streets. There were all sorts to learn from in Soweto: the rich and the poor, the leaders and the followers, the snails and the eagles, the good and the bad. Demonstrations against the apartheid government were intensifying, and there was a wave of 'crime' perpetrated by Blacks against Whites in the city. Black capitalists were emerging, the music was changing, labour unions were intensifying their strikes, and the Black Consciousness Movement was on the rise. 'So-where-to?' was what Sowetans jokingly called Soweto.

Soweto provided something that Sophiatown could not: lots of open spaces where kids would gather after school and on weekends to play. Soccer was the sport of choice for boys. This is where Mahobe would go after school and where his love of soccer began. There were many big-name soccer players to look up to. These players were not just famous athletes: they were gods in the townships. They were held in such high esteem that they came to be referred to by awe-inspiring nicknames that would eventually replace their first names entirely. The children would follow these players in the streets to get a chance to touch their mighty shoulders, or even just the fringes of the garments they were wearing. These heroes included the sensational Kaizer 'Chincha Guluva' Motaung, Thomas 'Zero My Hero' Johnson, Percy 'Chippa' Moloi, Bernard 'Dancing Shoes' Hartze, and Eric 'Scara' Sono, who, though he died tragically in a car crash in 1964, remained on the lips of many soccer fans for years afterwards. Many kids in Soweto named themselves after these idols, and 'Scara' and 'Chippa' became the most popular nicknames.

* * *

Mahobe attended secondary school at Meadowlands High in Soweto. He also played as a striker for a team in Meadowlands, going by the nickname 'Mauser', after the famous German rifle. But he enjoyed only modest success as a player, and soon realised that playing soccer was not going to quench his craving for fame and fortune.

Harrison Selulu was a big fan of Moroka Swallows, and he would take Mahobe and his friend with him to the stadium to look after his car while he watched the game. But the boys had other plans. They would always wait a moment before following silently behind him. They would watch him all the way until he reached his seat and seemed comfortable. Then they would find a place to sit behind him, out of sight but enjoying the game. They would make sure to sneak out before the game ended. He never caught them.

Unbeknown to him, Uncle Selulu was shaping Mahobe's life. Seeing those big games and the jubilant crowds at the stadiums brought something alive inside him. He wanted to be a part of it. He wanted to be a part of *them*. The two biggest Soweto clubs in those days were Orlando Pirates and Moroka Swallows. But it was Pirates who always set the pace, winning title after title. Mahobe was a true Pirates man. He used to relish the times when Pirates were playing and Uncle Selulu had not asked to be accompanied to a Swallows match. He would sneak out and go and watch the

Pirates match, telling his uncle that he was going to join the boys at the playgrounds. Fans came out in numbers to see Pirates, regardless of which team they were playing. Pirates had pierced his heart, just as they had pierced the hearts of many young boys and girls across Soweto.

After leaving school in 1971, Mahobe worked for an international company called Rank Xerox, which sold and serviced Xerox photocopiers. By this time, he had given up on a career as a soccer player, but he knew that soccer was where he belonged. It was going to be a part of his life, one way or the other. Even though South Africa had been suspended from the international football governing body, FIFA, way back in 1961, and was eventually expelled in 1976, soccer continued to thrive in the country. On match days, throngs of spectators streamed to township venues like Orlando Stadium in Soweto.

Interestingly, the Whites-only South African Football Association (SAFA), which was formed in 1892, was the first football association from outside of Europe to join FIFA, which it did in 1910. Subsequently, the English Football Association sent amateur representative sides to South Africa to play against Whites-only sides. South Africa was also one of the founding members of the Confederation of African Football (CAF) in 1957, together with Egypt, Sudan, and Ethiopia. In 1960, CAF expelled South Africa. The problem was apartheid and its injustices. FIFA was putting pressure on South Africa to abolish racism in soccer, and the sporting boycott of South Africa was a powerful weapon. The struggle for the racial integration of South African soccer was a microcosm of the overarching struggle for the racial integration of the people of South Africa and the fall of apartheid. Football sanctions were some of the very first international indictments of the apartheid regime, and they were paying dividends. Man shall not live by bread alone, but also by the happiness of the soul.

Soccer meant a lot to the Black people of South Africa during apartheid. It was a unifier – a way of holding on to humanity, to sanity. People could forget their troubles and laugh and dance and jump with joy as they watched their favourite teams in action. This was what inspired Mahobe – seeing those happy faces in the midst of pain and suffering, like little stars glowing and floating about in a storm of darkness. The African National Congress (ANC) had long recognised the significance of soccer in the lives of people and as a weapon against apartheid. Way back in 1944 they had sponsored the first soccer match at the Bantu Sports Club in Johannesburg, which comprised a club house, soccer fields, tennis courts, and a mini soccer stadium that sat 5 000 spectators. In 1946, Chief Albert Luthuli helped establish the Natal Inter-Race Soccer Board. Soccer continued to be intertwined with politics, and it provided a safe space for underground operatives of the liberation movement to meet. Many would emerge from hiding to attend matches and confer with fellow operatives at a soccer match. Soccer was also used to raise funds for the ANC, and some matches were organised specifically for this purpose.

* * *

Mahobe also loved the limelight that soccer brought to those who ran it. There were the big kahunas, the likes of Kaizer 'Chincha Guluva' Motaung, who had founded Kaizer Chiefs in 1970; the flamboyant and fast-talking Ewert 'The Lip' Nene, a cofounder of Kaizer Chiefs; and the larger-than-life Jack 'Big Daddy' Sello, who had funded the development of Moroka Swallows himself. These stars and others like them shone brightly and inspired millions of Black South Africans. These were the faces of Black Power, and Mahobe hankered after their glory.

Black Power was a slogan and an idea born out of the civil rights movement in the United States. It emphasised racial pride, economic empowerment, and the creation of political and cultural institutions. This had spilled over to South Africa because of the painful shared histories of the Black people of the two countries. James Brown's song 'Say it Loud, I'm Black and I'm Proud', which was released in August 1968, just months after the assassination of Martin Luther King, had become a Black Power anthem. Black Power also became associated with the rising of Black capitalists.

Mahobe's life gravitated more and more towards soccer. He also gravitated towards friends who loved soccer. Oh, and there was also money; he loved to keep company with friends who had money. That's where the good life was, and he could also learn a thing or two from them. His circle of friends included Simon 'Bra Six' Morake and Jabu 'Nyambose' Mthethwa. These were men-about-town who were snazzy dressers and had money. Like Mahobe, Mthethwa had experimented with becoming a soccer player, but had had only moderate success. They were big supporters of soccer and used to make sure that their favourite Pirates players' financial needs were taken care of. At the time, the top soccer bosses in Soweto were Kaizer Motaung and Jomo Sono, who owned their own teams. Of these, the guy who inspired Mahobe more and brought something alive in him was Motaung. Motaung was a former Orlando Pirates player whose mesmerising skills saw him sign with Atlanta Chiefs in the North American Soccer League in 1968. He came back to South Africa loaded with

US dollars and joined up with Thomas 'Zero' Johnson, Edward 'Msomi' Khoza and Ratha 'Jimmy Greaves' Mokgoatlheng, who had been expelled from Pirates, to form Kaizer Chiefs. Chiefs also recruited talented players such as Herman 'Pelé' Blaschke, midfield genius Patrick 'Ace' Ntsoelengoe, and many other talented players. Many soccer fans, including those from Pirates, started to switch allegiance and become Chiefs fans.

There was tension between Pirates fans and Chiefs fans that sometimes led to fights. Then Kaizer Chiefs coined the slogan 'Love and Peace'. It was their way of asking Pirates fans to stop the anger and violence against them. But it had a bigger context as well: it referred to what was happening in the country as a whole – a message to the apartheid oppressors to stop harassing people and let love and peace prevail.

'Love and Peace' was a version of the anti-war slogan 'Make Love Not War' used by Americans opposed to the war in Vietnam in the 1960s. The use of the slogan spread to issues relating to sexuality, human rights, traditional modes of authority, racial segregation, and White supremacy.

Kaizer Chiefs became a fashionable team, and the 'Love and Peace' philosophy was used to push the Kaizer Chiefs brand. Chiefs fans were also fashionable, and some of them used to wear bell-bottom pants and Afro hairstyles. This was the trend in America, where Motaung had played, and he brought the style back to South Africa when he returned. Bell-bottom pants were often worn skintight to the knee, then flared out in a wide soft drape. This dress sense was associated with popular American entertainers such as James Brown, husband-and-wife team Sonny and Cher, and Percy Sledge. But it was Percy Sledge and Kaizer Motaung who made bell-bottoms and Afros popular in South

Africa. Percy Sledge toured South Africa in 1970, and South Africans fell in love with not only his music but also his style. Everybody wanted to look like him and Kaizer Motaung.

Some of the Orlando Pirates fans regarded the bell-bottoms and Afro look as soft, almost feminine, and used to harass those who wore them. But most girls found the style sexy and loved the Chiefs guys. This look, combined with excellent soccer, propelled the Kaizer Chiefs brand to greater heights. They were not called the 'Phefeni Glamour Boys' for nothing. Phefeni, in Orlando West, was the place where Kaizer Motaung had grown up, and this was where it all started for Kaizer Chiefs.

The stylish flair and on-field wizardry of Kaizer Chiefs was beginning to make Pirates look a bit faded, and this was bad news for die-hard Pirates fans like Zola Mahobe. If only something could be done to bring back the glory days of Pirates, he thought. The same thought was running through the mind of Irvin Khoza, who saw Pirates as a big brand and dreamt of running the team one day. He was to later own it.

Snowy Moshoeshoe

— *Indoni yamanzi*

It was while working at Xerox that Mahobe met the beautiful Tebello Snowy Moshoeshoe. It was August 1976 and the Putco buses were not transporting workers to their places of work after the announcement of a nationwide three-day strike. The political atmosphere was still highly charged in Soweto, following the Soweto student uprising of June that year, which had changed the socio-political landscape in South Africa.

The previous day, 23 August, young Black demonstrators in Soweto had stoned buses and trains to force compliance with the strike. Police shot and killed one Black youth and wounded at least six others. As many as 80 per cent of Black workers did not turn up for work in many factories. Pamphlets promoting the strike bore the slogan *'Azikhwelwa'*, meaning 'We will not ride'. Many trains to Johannesburg were cancelled, and those that ran were almost empty. After many of their buses were stoned, the Putco Bus Company ordered its drivers to halt at the Soweto boundary and not continue any further.

Mahobe and his friends, dressed in fancy clothes and driving in a Chevrolet Impala convertible – an eyeful of a car – stopped at a petrol station in Orlando. Mahobe went into the shop to buy some drinks. It was one of very few petrol stations open that day; most were closed as a precautionary measure.

As he was about to be served, his whole world came to a standstill. Entering the shop was Snowy Moshoeshoe. She was with her friend, Gladys, who was her neighbour in Orlando East, where she lived. The two always dressed up when going to the shops. It was a Soweto thing – girls loved to dress up whenever they left the house.

He could not stop looking at her. As he stared at her delicate face and captivating smile, he was transported to another world, suddenly oblivious to the one he was in.

'*Bhuti*, I am still waiting for you to pay; you are slowing down the queue,' said the cashier to him.

'Oh, *ngiyaxolisa sisi wami*,' he said as he fumbled in his pockets and handed her the money, dropping some coins on the floor as he did so. He did not bother to pick them up.

'You guys just wait here; there is something I need to take care of,' he said to his friends when he got to the car. And off he went as if driven by some invisible wind.

* * *

Snowy was quiet and reserved and, on the surface, the complete opposite of Mahobe, who was more of an extrovert, learning fast from the University of Life. She knew how to express her femininity – she was quietly confident, elegantly simple, and sparingly provocative. She had an enigmatic smile that lingered in his mind and seemed to pierce his soul.

At that time, she was finishing high school. She was attracted to Mahobe, but doubted his motives. He surrounded himself with 'businessmen' and other know-it-alls of Soweto who, like the Americans of Sophiatown, were 'players' and dressed in fancy clothes and drove flashy cars. Players never change, she thought to herself. What if she was just a trophy to him?

'*Mngani wami*, you don't know how lucky you are,' said Gladys. 'Many girls would give the world to be in your shoes. It is not every day that you get a guy like that begging for your love. If you don't want him, you can always toss him over to me.'

'That's not how this game is played, *mngani*, haibo!'

'You will never know if you don't give him a chance. Anyway, if you don't want him, I hope he turns this way.'

* * *

The harder Snowy tried to discourage Mahobe, the more determined he was to go after her. 'Life is a big chase, my broer,' one of his know-it-all friends had once said to him. 'When a hunter is in the bush hunting, and he comes across a nice, plump little buck just standing there shouting, "Kill me! Kill me! Have my meat!" does he stop the hunt to take home what is offered so easily? No, he passes by and goes after that elusive one – the one that he is not even sure he will take home. The excitement of the hunt is in the hunting.' But it was more than a hunt for him; Cupid's arrow had pierced his heart. As she got to know him better, Snowy slowly let go of her defences and doubts and began to let him more and more into her life.

'Are you sure Zola is your kind of guy, *mngani*? The two of you seem so different,' said Gladys one day as they enjoyed a cake that Mahobe had brought for Snowy. The cake had also come with flowers and a card expressing his love for her.

'I don't know, but something inside of me likes him. I think I could get along with him.'

'If I were you, I would still be careful, though. Just don't rush things.'

'My eyes are wide open, *mngani*.'

'I'm still not sure the two of you belong together though.'

'Come on, now, let's not spoil the mood. Let's enjoy the cake.'

'Just saying. Anyway, you're right. I wish I could have a guy who brings me flowers.'

'Don't worry, you will find him one day.'

* * *

After matriculating, Snowy trained as a nurse and then began working at Leratong Hospital in the west of Johannesburg. Nursing was one of the few prestigious professions in those days, as not many people got to have a post-school formal qualification. Nurses were elevated to half-doctor status and were well respected in their communities. They were indeed half doctors to many community members, and often used to assist in home births. Gladys, on the other hand, found a job at Standard Bank and trained as a bank clerk. The two continued to be friends, but Mahobe was beginning to replace Gladys in Snowy's life. Lately, they were not spending so much time together.

'*Mngani*, do you think you can connect me with one of Zola's friends?' Gladys asked Snowy as they enjoyed some Indian food at Kapitan's Café in Fordsburg – one of the few multiracial restaurants during apartheid. 'I need a guy in my life,' she continued. 'Besides, if I go out with one of Zola's friends, we will be able to continue to do things together, like double dating or going on trips together. What do you say?'

'Actually, it would not be a bad idea. Let me think ... apart from Zola, the only guy that seems promising is Stix. The others are just Casanovas. What do you think of him?'

'What's funny is that I was actually thinking of him. I think I like him. Can you organise it, my friend?'

'I'll make a plan.'

It did not take long for Snowy to arrange a little get-together to which both Gladys and Stix were invited. With a little nudge from Mahobe and Snowy, Stix soon found himself spending more and more time with Gladys, and before he knew it, he had developed romantic feelings for her. But it was still Mahobe who would have been her number one choice, if she could have had her way.

Studying the system
– *Uvukile wazenzela*

Mahobe needed to make money – big money – to make his dreams come true, and he was not going to make it by staying at Xerox. He needed a job that would develop him, so that he would eventually be able to start a meaningful business. In 1981, he left Xerox to join IBM, a computer company operating from the city centre in Johannesburg. IBM was a small cog in the apartheid wheel, enabling military operations and other oppressive practices that involved using computers, yet it was also one of the first companies to allow Black people to hold positions in accounting, planning, warehousing, maintenance, and other important areas. From the late 1970s, it began to actively recruit and train Blacks, especially as systems engineers.

It was prestigious working for IBM in those days. Working on computers was a new thing and was associated with intelligence. Those who got the opportunity to join IBM were envied by their peers. It also held the promise of a better living. Blacks employed by IBM were reported to earn twice as much as Blacks employed in similar positions elsewhere.

One of IBM's big clients was Standard Bank, whose information systems ran on IBM technology. It was while working there that Mahobe learnt to code computer programs in the software used by Standard Bank. It was not part of his job description to know about the systems of Standard Bank, but he had managed to sneak out photocopies of relevant training manuals, which he would spend many long nights studying. It was not difficult sneaking out the manuals; in those days, Black people whose jobs made them feel important used to carry briefcases to work, even if there was only a *skaftin* (lunch box) inside.

There were ideas taking shape in Mahobe's head as he studied the manuals, like pieces of a puzzle falling together. His senses became sharpened and his curiosity grew. He wanted to know more. There was something there that he could use.

* * *

After a year, he had learned everything he wanted to learn at IBM. It was time to move on and do something with the wealth of knowledge that he had acquired. He duly left the company to join Standard Bank in Jabulani, Soweto. He was charming and bold, and he befriended his White colleagues who were responsible for the computer processes involving client accounts. He knew a lot about soccer and would discuss the English Premier League matches with them, as well as popular players of the time. He would sometimes even sit with them in their offices during lunchtime. In-between, he would subtly ask questions; not directly, but in such a manner that they would disclose information without realising they were doing so.

'So what happens if the computer registers a transaction but there is no paperwork to back it up?' he would ask. 'What if the computer statement does not match the paperwork in the client's file? Is it possible to reverse a transaction? Do transactions that have been reversed reflect on the client's statement?'

There were no ATMs and no mobile banking systems back then, meaning that bank clients could only access their account statements by going to the bank during working hours, which rarely happened. Normally, clients received their statements once a month by mail. Mahobe would look for opportunities to learn more about the computer systems: what was possible and what was not. On Saturdays, when some of his White colleagues were off, he would sneak into their offices and work with the computers. He picked his moments well and nobody noticed, as they were used to seeing him go in and out of these offices.

* * *

In 1983, he decided to leave the bank to start his own computer business, Power Promotions. The new age of personal computing had just begun, with the release of the ZX Spectrum in 1982 – an extremely basic computer by modern standards. However, it was soon followed by others, such as the Commodore, which marketing boffins called the wonder computer of the 1980s. Power Promotions sold computers and also helped clients with computer programming. There was a market for computers among the affluent Blacks in South Africa, as well as in Black businesses.

Mahobe then convinced Snowy to leave her nursing job at Leratong Hospital and seek a job at Standard Bank. With help from Gladys, she got the job. Standard Bank, originally called Standard Bank of British South Africa, was one of the largest banks in South Africa. It was the first bank to have a branch in Johannesburg, around 1886. In the 1980s, Standard Bank was one of the top two banks in South Africa, the other being Barclays Bank, which was renamed First National Bank (FNB) in 1987.

Snowy's job at the bank was in the cheque clearance centre at Head Office, and her banking chores were done on computers. They trained her, but it was Mahobe who taught her most of what she needed to know. She did well in the job, learnt quickly, and was much valued by the bank.

There was money – lots of it – just sitting there in the bank, waiting to be taken, Mahobe explained to her. She could become rich – they could become rich – if only she had the guts to go along with his plan. 'Just close your eyes and think of it, my love. Just imagine all the nice things we can have: nice cars, nice houses, travelling around the world and sipping champagne. You could wear the best shoes in Soweto. No, you could wear the best shoes this side of the world.'

'It's very tempting,' she said, 'but don't tell me you're serious about it.'

'Oh yes, I'm dead serious.'

'What about if we get caught; what happens to us then?'

'There is no way they are going to catch us, I promise. I have covered every angle and even did tests when I was working at Jabulani Standard Bank; there is no way they can catch us if we are careful.'

'What if I can't go ahead with it?'

'Then I will find another way.'

'No, my love, you can't involve someone else. People can't be trusted. I will help you.'

'Did I hear you right?' said Mahobe. 'Did you just say that you will help me?'

'Yes, I'll help you.'

'You don't know what that means to me. Come here,' he said, holding her tight for what seemed like forever.

'There is more,' he whispered into her ear. Then he released her from his arms, sat up straight, put his hand on his knees and looked the other way. There was an awkward moment of silence.

'It sounds serious,' she said, breaking the silence.

'Yes, it is serious; and if it can't be done then we can't take the money.'

'Ok, out with it. What is it?'

'Where do I start? All I can say is that it is going to involve the forging of signatures. We'll set up many bank accounts belonging to my businesses, as well as some belonging to non-existent people, except those people will be us. The paperwork will have to be in place, with signed documents and cheques. Sometimes these businesses will pay money into the Power Promotions account and the accounts of my other businesses. Some of the money will be paid into accounts controlled by you. There is money, my love – money beyond your wildest imagination. Standard Bank can become our bottomless pit of money; there for us anytime we want it. What do you say? Can you do that? We will practise day and night until you get it right.'

'I will do anything for you, my love.'

'And I will do anything for you.'

His fingers reached up to trace the contours of her lips. Then he held her tight and sealed it with a kiss.

'The world is now on one side and we are on the other side. There is a line in-between that cannot be crossed. We cannot cross it, and neither should we allow the world to cross it.'

So began the journey of Zola Mahobe and Snowy Moshoeshoe, mavericks who were about to embark on the biggest and most sophisticated bank robbery South Africa had ever seen. No guns, no forcing the safes open, no intimidating anyone in the bank; just two invisible people who would take the money whenever they wished.

Nobody knew about their scheme except the two of them. Their relationship had grown from that of lovers to that of confidantes and 'business partners'. Snowy also loved the attention she got from him for her boldness, and she was willing to do anything for him. But the same was true for Mahobe – he loved the attention he got from her for his whip-smart ways of doing business and his ability to dream big. They were under each other's spell, inseparable.

* * *

Mahobe's relationship with Snowy was complicated. He had another girlfriend, Siza, whom he eventually married, although he continued to stay with Snowy. Snowy and everybody else around Mahobe knew about Siza. He also had a girlfriend, Mandisa, from Transkei, and she was the mother of his first child. Snowy also knew about this girlfriend. Siza was the one many Sowetans knew about, and they used to puzzle over why Mahobe continued to maintain the marriage while he was staying full-time with another woman. They were also puzzled by the fact that Siza continued to be Mrs Mahobe when her husband was living with another woman. He provided well for her, however, and made sure that she had no reasons to complain about money. It was not uncommon for guys with money to have more than one woman. Money could get you what you liked. To all intents and purposes, Snowy was also his wife. According to Sipho Mahlaba, who at one stage lived in the same house as Mahobe and Snowy in Rockville, Soweto: 'Snowy knew who Zola was and knew that he loved her more than any of the other women in his life. They were soulmates, and he spent most of his time with her. Their affair was public knowledge and whenever he was seen with a woman, it was with her.'

Playing politics

– *Uboshiwe eJohnVorster*

The name 'Power Promotions' was not only an expression of personal ambition for Mahobe, but was also about promoting Black Power. He was sympathetic towards the Black liberation movement, and his brother was a member of the Pan Africanist Congress (PAC). With Mahobe's help, this brother eventually skipped the country to join the Azanian People's Liberation Army (APLA), which was the armed wing of the PAC. Many young South Africans at the time believed that the armed struggle was the only way to liberate the people of South Africa. Those in APLA were willing to take on the apartheid regime, and they later adopted the rallying cry 'One Settler, One Bullet'.

Mahobe worked underground for the PAC, helping members to cross borders into South Africa or out to neighbouring countries, using his money and connections. He had connections in Lesotho, Zimbabwe, Swaziland and Botswana – businesspeople whom nobody suspected of being involved in politics.

For his troubles, he was once arrested and interrogated for a few weeks at the infamous John Vorster Square, a place where comrades used to mysteriously fall out of windows or trip down stairs and into nooses. But he was too slick for the authorities – they found no concrete proof of his involvement.

'There was this PAC lady comrade of Zola's who used to stay in Pimville, Soweto,' explained Sipho Mahlaba. 'Together they used to use one of those old Volkswagen Kombis with curtains as a disguise when they were transporting the PAC guys. People thought that Zola was just being funny by owning the Kombi. It was old and slow, and no one expected anybody on a get-away-fast mission to use such a vehicle. It was a perfect decoy.

'She left the country a month or so before Zola got detained at John Vorster Square. At least, she never came back to Pimville. Maybe she was killed; maybe she is still alive and is a big shot somewhere in government – I don't know.'

It was not surprising that Mahobe was involved in politics. Every Black person, and every White person for that matter, was involved in politics in one form or another. There are many unacknowledged people who played important and sometimes dangerous roles in the struggle against apartheid, some of whom paid the ultimate price.

Detention without trial was introduced in 1963 and provided for detention in isolation, without access to the courts, for 90 days for the purposes of interrogation. The 90-day detention was renewable upon expiry, meaning that people could be detained for months on end without access to the courts. Other Acts followed, but it was the Internal Security Amendment Act (Act 79 of 1976), which was introduced following the Soweto student uprising in 1976, that became the most widely recognised. The Act was introduced to withdraw political activists from the political arena. According to this Act, people could be detained without trial for up to twelve months, renewable. It has been estimated that up to 80 000 people were detained at John Vorster Square, some of whom were held for more than 850 days.

* * *

When he was released from John Vorster Square, Mahobe went to stay at the house in Pimville that belonged to his PAC comrade, since she was no longer staying there and the house had been empty for a while. The main reason he went to stay there was that Siza, his wife, was expecting his second child. They stayed there together.

In those days, there were inspectors who came to inspect the houses in the townships, especially those issued through companies that Black people worked for. When they arrived at the house, they found the garden in a terrible state. Mahobe and Siza were young and busy and neither of them had time to look after the garden. All they were doing was making sure that the rent was always paid. The inspectors threatened to evict him and sell the house, but he pleaded with them, using Siza's pregnancy to appeal to their emotions, and promised he would make sure the house and its surrounds were clean. They came back some weeks later and gave him an ultimatum to buy the house, upon which he went to the offices of the authorities and did so.

* * *

Mandisa was also very beautiful. It was while he was at John Vorster Square that she decided to leave him. It was a scary place, John Vorster Square, and things were not looking good for Mahobe. He had already had a child with her – his first – before he had the second with Siza. She was now pregnant with his third child (his second with her).

About three years later, out of the blue, she asked to see Mahobe. She brought the child with her – a boy who was a little more than two years old. They met in town near the Carlton Centre and decided to sit in his car to talk. After a while, she got out of the car and told him she was just going to get something from the bakery nearby and would be back shortly. But she never returned. Instead, she got into the car of her new boyfriend and off they went. Mahobe had to go home with the child.

The child lived with Mahobe and Snowy in Central, Soweto. Snowy was fine with it; in fact, she was happy to have the child in the house and enjoyed being part of a family. At that time, Mahobe and Siza were no longer staying together; he had left her to live with Snowy again.

One day a few years later, Mandisa's aunts and uncles arrived unannounced in about three cars. They found Snowy alone with the child. They introduced themselves as the boy's real family and told her they had come to fetch him. Snowy panicked and decided to call Mahobe. When he arrived, they told him that they had come to fetch their child. Mahobe tried to convince them that the boy was happy living with him and Snowy and was fond of them, and that it would be best for him to continue staying with them, but they would not budge. According to tradition the child belonged to them because Mahobe was not married to his mother.

Tradition won, and they handed the child over to the aunts and uncles. Snowy was devastated and so was the boy. She had grown fond of him and was raising him as her own and Mahobe's. With him around, the 'family' was complete.

Mandisa was nowhere to be seen in all of this; she never made any contact with Mahobe. She finally made an appearance a few years later, when Mahobe was famous. One day she just showed up at Mahobe's offices and started pleading with him to include her in his life, trying to use the children to soften him up. She eventually confessed that the second child was his. He accepted responsibility for the children but refused to take her back. Later, he had another child with Siza – their second, and child number four for him.

Mr Cool, Mr Big Bucks
– *Imali eningi*

As soon as Snowy joined Standard Bank, they put their plan into motion. Snowy became Mahobe's bank manager, managing the many fictitious accounts they set up. His businesses started to grow. Apart from Power Promotions, he also had a butchery on Jeppe Street. Then he bought a liquor store in Johannesburg and another in Pietersburg (now Polokwane). He also bought a hotel next to Turfloop University (now the University of Limpopo) in Pietersburg. His liquor stores operated under the licence of his company Virgin Isle Liquor Outlet. He also owned a property company called ZM Property Holdings (ZM being his initials). The registered offices for these businesses were in Factor House on Kruis Street, Marshalltown, Johannesburg. He was the sole proprietor of both companies. He also owned liquor stores in Durban and Botswana. He did not register all of these businesses in his or Snowy's name; rather, he put some in the names of his friends.

Businesses such as butcheries, liquor stores, and other shops were some of the few types of businesses that Black people could own under apartheid. Denying Blacks opportunities in education was another one of apartheid's biggest weapons. Black people, according to the architects of apartheid, were there to serve White people. Blacks were therefore not allowed to go beyond certain levels of education or do certain degrees. In his speech in the South African Senate in 1954, Hendrik Verwoerd, then Minister of Native Affairs, declared:

> Up till now he [the Bantu] has been subjected to a school system which drew him away from his own community and practically misled him by showing him the green pastures of the European but still did not allow him to graze there ... It is abundantly clear that unplanned education creates many problems, disrupts the communal life of the Bantu and endangers the communal life of the European.

Black people were thus to be guided to participate in their own communities and not the White communities, as there was no place for them there. Therefore, even businesses that Black people owned were meant to serve only their own communities.

Mahobe ran his empire from the Power Promotions offices on Eloff Street in Johannesburg. Eloff Street and the area around it was the hub of Johannesburg back then. It was the grandest shopping street in the city.

**

* * *

Zola Mahobe had arrived. One minute no one had heard of him, and the next his name was on everybody's lips. His empire was growing at an alarming rate – the too-good-to-be-true kind of rate. He started buying expensive cars and mingling with A-list celebrities. He owned properties in Soweto and a luxury flat in Rosebank. Some referred to him as Mr Cool and others called him Mr Big Bucks, as he cultivated this image with his Afro hairstyle, open-neck shirts, rings and gold necklaces. Some affectionately referred to him as *Ophethe insimbi*, meaning one who is financially loaded.

When his 'rich' friends bought 190-series Mercedes-Benzes, which made a serious statement of wealth and status in the Black communities in those days, he bought himself a Mercedes-Benz 500 SL convertible – a cut above the rest. No other Sowetan owned a brand-new 500 SL convertible, or even an old 500 SL convertible, for that matter. He also bought Uncle Selulu a better car.

Snowy, on the other hand, did not drive a flashy car to work. 'Let sleeping dogs lie, my love; let them lie and even snore,' Mahobe liked saying to her.

'And they will lie, my love; no need to cause a disturbance,' she would say. But on weekends she was the belle of Soweto and the envy of many a woman.

* * *

'My friend, are you sure all of Zola's money is legit?' asked Gladys one day. She and Snowy were enjoying some Indian food at their favourite hangout, Kapitan's Café in Fordsburg.

'I am sure it is. Why do you ask?' The question had taken her by surprise.

'It's just that the way he is expanding his businesses and spending money on himself and his friends makes you wonder. I wish I could see his bank statements.'

'Don't think such thoughts, *mngani*. Where else would the money be coming from?'

'I don't know, but something doesn't add up. And you know, I am not the only one who thinks so.' She was right about that; many people were beginning to ask questions.

'I am sure you are just imagining things,' said Snowy. 'Zola is a very hard worker.'

'I am still not convinced. You must watch out, *mngani*. If I were you, I would not get too comfortable in your paradise. It could be short-lived.'

'Now I know you are just jealous.'

Even though Snowy and Gladys continued to be friends, there was an unspoken war going on between them. Snowy knew that Gladys was not completely over her feelings for Mahobe and that she was jealous of their relationship. She was always quick to criticise when something seemed to go wrong between them, and she was fond of making subtle comments about how she thought Mahobe was too streetwise for her. 'Actually, Zola is more suited to a girl like me than to you,' she would say.

Even Stix was beginning to get annoyed with Gladys's obsession with Mahobe. He knew that she would rather have him as her boyfriend, even though she always denied it. She never stopped talking about him.

'Sweetheart, should we always be talking about Zola and Snowy? Why are you so negative about their relationship?'

'It's just that I don't think they are suited for each other.'

'Don't you think you're involving yourself a little bit too much in their relationship? Zola loves Snowy and Snowy loves him. I don't see anything wrong about that.'

'No, sweetheart; Zola is not her kind of guy – he is more suited to someone like me.'

'So you keep saying. So why are you with me and not with him?'

'What do you mean by that?'

'To tell you the truth, your obsession with him makes me feel like a second-choice boyfriend.'

'Now you're just being insecure,' said Gladys sweetly. 'I'm only making an observation. You're the one for me. Promise.'

Stix sighed and walked away. He knew where her feelings lay, no matter what pleasant lies she told him.

* * *

Whenever he appeared at glamourous events, Mahobe was always accompanied by the beautiful and stylish Snowy Moshoeshoe. The two of them stood out. They both loved the attention of the media, which seemed to follow them wherever they went. Snowy came from modest means but had a penchant for beautiful shoes. It added to her mystique that she also claimed to be related to the King of Lesotho, King Moshoeshoe II, thus warding off questions about how she could afford such a lavish lifestyle. Nobody disputed her claims, and nobody tried to verify them.

What also worked in her favour was that she was not a hang-around-with-the-girls type of girl. She did not have many friends. At home they were a close-knit family that kept to itself and avoided the prying eyes and eavesdropping ears of the neighbours. This worked well for her. It made it easier for her to conceal her secrets. She could not afford to let anybody get close enough to her to get even a whiff of what she and Mahobe were up to.

While people were still awestruck by Mohobe's sudden fame and fortune, he and Snowy started travelling the world, mostly to countries big on soccer such as Brazil, Italy, Germany and England. They also loved holidaying on islands such as the Seychelles and Mauritius. He even started his own travel agency, called Via Africa Travel Agents.

Then he bought a racehorse and became the first Black member of the Newmarket Race Club in Alberton, a White suburb situated on the East Rand. He kept his horse in Khayalami, where they groomed and trained it. On race days, the masters and madams of Johannesburg's high society would descend in a flurry of elaborate headgear and fancy frocks to enjoy a day in the sun. Mahobe and Snowy, the only Blacks there, would be with them. Not to be outdone, the finely dressed gentlemen would also show off their jazzy suits for the occasion. It was a place of merrymaking, friendship and networking. Champagne would flow, especially for those who had won a bet or whose horses had done well. There would be lots of celebrations and hugging. Mahobe made a lot of White friends at the club, some of whom became his business partners.

Mahobe was a nonconformist. By becoming the first Black member of the race club, he was symbolising the breaking down of the barriers of racism in South Africa. Even though this was during the time when Blacks who mingled with Whites were viewed suspiciously by fellow Blacks, who accused them of selling out or being apartheid spies, this did not deter him. They would soon understand. He was a maverick, stepping into uncharted territory.

He was accepted and welcomed with open arms at the club. The truth was that even though the apartheid laws forbade it, Blacks and Whites did mingle at certain levels, either as comrades, business partners, fellow artists, friends, or even lovers. Mahobe was just taking this to the public arena. The club operated until 24 May 2001, when it was officially announced that the bell had tolled for horse racing in Alberton, exactly 63 years after it had all started, back in 1938.

He then bought himself a game farm called Ninja Game Farm in Bushbuckridge, Mpumalanga, and registered it under the name of a White business partner, Benny Len. Benny Len and Elio Rossi, another of his business partners, were two of the many White friends whom he had met at Newmarket Race Club. The property in Rosebank was also registered under Benny Len's name.

Many people were baffled by his deep pockets. There seemed to be no end to his spending spree. Some suspected that there was something immoral about his wealth, while others believed it had been justly earned. 'I have made a lot of ground in business because I don't hesitate when I want something,' he used to say, speaking in a riddle. He treated his employees well and gave his friends top positions in his businesses. His motto was 'Let everybody be happy, then the money will flow in.' And flow in it did.

Mahobe also gave unstintingly to the needy, and even built houses for his friends and staff members in Soweto, Mamelodi and Eersterust, east of Pretoria. He also often paid school fees for children from struggling families, and even paid for university education for some. He became extremely popular in the Soweto community.

Paying tribute to him, Jan 'Malombo' Lechaba, the former Sundowns and Chiefs midfielder, said, 'Zola did not want to see people suffer, especially the poor. He was a humble man who was more concerned about upgrading the lives of others.

According to Sipho Mahlaba, 'He was like Mandela when it came to children. If Zola saw a kid crying in the street, he would stop his car and ask what was happening and help where he could. I think it was his poor upbringing as a child that made him care for kids so much.'

He was a paragon of generosity. 'Love thy neighbour as thyself' seemed to be engraved on the tablet of his heart. He also used to tip generously, and would give anything between R80 and R200 to the boys who used to wash his cars. That was a lot of money in the 1980s.

* * *

The Orlando Pirates players were like family to Mahobe. Apart from being household names in Soweto, and indeed across the whole of South Africa and in neighbouring countries like Namibia, he had also grown up with some of them. His rich friends were also Pirates supporters and used to mingle with the players at parties, especially those held after a big Pirates win. This gave him an opportunity to befriend the players. As soon as the money started to flow, he began financially supporting Orlando Pirates. He also treated Pirates players as though they were his players – almost as if he were the custodian of the team. Some of them went to him for help with personal financial problems, and he gave them the money they needed without expecting it to be paid back. He even encouraged them to come back should the need arise – as long as they kept on playing for Pirates.

At that time, in the 1980s, no single person or group of people owned Orlando Pirates. It was a community team registered as a non-governmental organisation (NGO). The team was formed way back in 1937 by mine workers who had settled in the east of Orlando in Soweto. Many had migrated from rural KwaZulu, Natal, the northern Transvaal and the Orange Free State (now KwaZulu-Natal, Limpopo and the Free State) to seek better job opportunities in the big city of Johannesburg. The team was first called the Orlando Boys Club, but this changed to Orlando Pirates somewhere around 1939/40 under their first president, Bethuel Mokgosinyana.

Mahobe was ready for his next acquisition, and he had his sights set on Pirates. He approached the Pirates administration and offered to buy the team, but they refused. They explained that they had also turned down another offer from former Pirates player Jomo Sono. 'Orlando Pirates does not belong to any single person; it belongs to the people of Orlando,' they told him.

Sono went on to purchase the status (franchise) of Dion Highlands Park Football Club (FC), a historically White club from Pretoria, for R100 000. He renamed it Dion Cosmos in its initial (1983) season. The first part of the name represented the previous sponsor of Highlands Park – Dion – and the second part was his fingerprint: he decided to name it after his former club in the US, the New York Cosmos. In 1984, Dion Cosmos was renamed Jomo Cosmos. Naming the club after himself and the club that he had played for in the US was a trend set by the founder of Kaizer Chiefs, Kaizer Motaung, who named his team after himself and the Atlanta Chiefs. Motaung went further, though: he even based the Kaizer Chiefs logo on the Atlanta Chiefs emblem.

Of course, Mahobe knew that Pirates belonged to the Orlando community, but to him it made perfect sense for the team to become a company and not an NGO. After all, there was already a debate in the Orlando Pirates camp about turning it into a company. He did not plan to move it from Orlando – it was still going to belong to the people. He suspected there was another reason behind the refusal to sell.

There are those who have suggested that Irvin Khoza, who had earlier been part of the Orlando Pirates establishment, already had his eye on owning Pirates. Khoza does not deny that he had dreams of running Orlando Pirates. Once, in 1968, while watching a Pirates game with Dan Lebowa, he told him that they were going to run the club one day.

However, Khoza was not part of Orlando Pirates at the time Mahobe made his offer to buy the club, as he had been expelled for reasons that have never been made clear. But he still had one foot in the club and kept helping out the team financially. In those days, rich Black 'businessmen' contributed in whatever way they could, including supporting clubs and individual players financially, even if they were not officially attached to the clubs. Ironically, in 1991, when Khoza took over all administration of the club, he registered it as Orlando Pirates FC (Pty) Ltd, which is exactly what Mahobe had had in mind. He became chairman of the club in 1992.

It seems there was a battle for the soul of Orlando Pirates going on between Mahobe and Khoza. Not really a battle, more like a yearning – a felt obligation – to nurse Pirates back to good health. The team was struggling at the time, mainly because of internal politics. They both genuinely loved the club and supported it however they could, but Mahobe was a man on the move and wanted action now. He had the money, the love and the passion – and he was ready to take over. But Khoza was patient; he understood the situation at Pirates better, and he knew they needed someone like him to stabilise the club.

After being turned down by Orlando Pirates, the intrepid Mahobe went hunting for another team to buy. But his strategy had to change. He was not interested in any of the big Soweto clubs apart from Orlando Pirates, so he did not bid for shares in either Moroka Swallows or Kaizer Chiefs. He instead bought shares in a small second division club called Botafogo FC, named after the then-famous Brazilian football club Botafogo.

Mahobe's Botafogo FC was just limping along, as was the case with many second division clubs back then, and most of the players did not have the proper attire for training and playing matches. He bought them soccer boots, tracksuits and uniforms. He even bailed out individual players from his own pocket, without expecting any of the money to be paid back.

He was a man on a mission and soon became a favourite with players. But an ominous cloud hung in the air. When his co-owner saw his popularity with the players, he started feeling insecure, since he felt that control of the team was slipping away from him. He started questioning most of the decisions that Mahobe made in order to frustrate his ambitions, and they quarrelled often.

Mahobe decided to relinquish his shareholding in Botafogo FC to look for another team. It was a great loss to the players, who were beginning to see the light under his stewardship. His leaving marked the beginning of the end for Botafogo.

Following this disappointment, he went on the hunt again. He had his ear to the ground, listening out for any interesting developments on the soccer scene. There was a club in Pretoria called Mamelodi Sundowns that had earned promotion to the first division of the National Professional Soccer League but had been struggling. The club was also struggling in the newly formed National Soccer League, which had replaced the National Professional Soccer League, and was hovering at the tail end of the log. It needed saving, and Mahobe was brought in by the owners to negotiate its purchase.

The early days of Mamelodi Sundowns

– *Umlando*

Mamelodi Sundowns FC had its roots in Marabastad, a cosmopolitan area near the Pretoria city centre. Marabastad was a culturally diverse area occupied mainly by Blacks, Coloureds and Indians until the enactment of the Group Areas Act of 1950, which was intended to remove non-Whites residing in settlements on the fringes of the cities to the areas designated for their race groups. Marabastad's Black residents were relocated to Atteridgeville between 1940 and 1950, the Coloured residents were sent to Eersterust between 1962 and 1965, and the Indian residents were packed off to Laudium and Claudius between 1960 and 1976. Unlike Sophiatown, Marabastad was not reduced to rubble but retained many of its original buildings and became primarily a business district, with most of the shops owned by Indians, some of whom had lived there and already owned businesses there before the forced removals.

The history of Mamelodi Sundowns is sketchy, but evidence suggests that it was originally formed as an amateur club in the 1940s and named Pretoria Sundowns. The club was renamed Marabastad Sundowns in the early 1960s. It is not clear what prompted the name change or how ownership of the club was affected. According to the Sundowns website, the club was originally formed by a group of 'young stars' who called Marabastad their home, but it was not an official professional league club affiliated to any soccer federation. Among these young stars, the club mentions Frank 'ABC' Motsepe, Roy Fischer, Ingle Singh and Bernard 'Dancing Shoes' Hartze. Hartze went on to become one of the first players to play professionally across racial lines when he joined Orlando Pirates in 1967. This was until the National Professional Soccer League, a league for Black players, instructed Black clubs to deregister Coloured and Indian players in 1969/70. Hartze subsequently joined Cape Town Spurs, where in 1972 he set the South African record for a single-season goal-scoring average by scoring 35 goals in 16 matches.

Ingle Singh and Roy Fischer went on to help Kaizer Motaung form the Kaizer XI and became some of its first players. Singh played a few games for Chiefs and then went back to Sundowns, where he played until he retired. After that, he became the manager of the team.

Frank Motsepe – not to be confused with his brother, Chief Augustine Butana Chaane (ABC) Motsepe, father of the current owner of Mamelodi Sundowns, Patrice Motsepe – is said to have gone on to play for Pretoria Spa Sporting FC in the latter half of the 1960s. At Pretoria Spa Sporting, Frank also played alongside a young Kgalema Motlanthe, who much later would become president of South Africa. Motlanthe had moved to

Atteridgeville from Meadowlands in Soweto, where he had played for Meadowlands Spa FC. Pretoria Spa Sporting was one of the teams in the Atteridgeville Football Association League.

Marabastad Sundowns was a popular club in the city and surrounding areas and attracted large crowds to their home ground, which was in the traditionally Muslim part of Marabastad. Fans did not mind catching the train from Mamelodi, getting off at the Pretoria West train station, and walking to the ground.

When a fruit market was built where the Muslim ground stood, Sundowns were deprived of a venue, so the club relocated to the Coloured area of Eersterust. This would turn out to be a costly move for them as it became more and more difficult to keep the players and attract the kinds of crowds they had attracted in Marabastad.

* * *

Marabastad Sundowns became an official club in 1970 and was affiliated with the Federation Professional League (FPL) in 1973. The FPL was a South African league that was established to allow Coloured and Indian players to play competitively under the sports segregation laws. The FPL was affiliated with the South African Soccer Federation (SASF), which was an anti-apartheid soccer federation formed by Blacks, Indians and Coloureds.

In 1976, Marabastad Sundowns reached the finals of the FPL version of the Coca-Cola Shield Cup, where they played against Berea FC at Curries Fountain Stadium in Durban. They drew the match 3–3, with Berea winning the replay. The line-up comprised Indian and Coloured players.

At that time there were a number of professional soccer leagues in operation in South Africa. Apartheid imposed itself on everything that South Africans did, and even though soccer leagues strived to be nonracial, they could not be. There was the Whites-only National Football League (NFL), which was founded in 1959 and was the country's first entirely professional club league. The National Professional Soccer League (NPSL), which was for Blacks, was founded in 1961. It folded the following year and was resurrected in 1967. It was reorganised into the 'African' league in 1971. Coloureds and Indians competed in the FPL, founded in 1969.

These leagues were not designed to compete against one another, but there was nevertheless competition between them, and the bottom line was spectator entertainment value. Signs of racial integration were also beginning to show and, just like in politics at the time, there was a battle going on to determine who was going to swallow up the others and emerge on top as the dominant league in South African football.

The NFL attracted good crowds to the stadiums during the years 1959 to 1969, but attendance began to decline in the early 1970s. In an effort to keep the spectators interested, NFL team bosses resorted to importing well-known international star players such as Gordon Banks, Roger Hunt, Francis Lee, Geoff Hurst, Bobby Moore, George Best and Bobby Charlton, to name but a few, on short contracts. Even though they were slightly past their peak, they were still excellent players and very popular. Most of them had been members of the England team that won the 1966 World Cup, beating West Germany 4–2.

Gordon Banks played as goalkeeper, had 73 caps for England, and had been named FIFA goalkeeper of the year on six occasions.

Banks was mostly remembered for his spectacular save that denied the great Pele of Brazil a goal in the 1970 FIFA World Cup. That save has been dubbed 'the greatest save of the century'. So much influence did Gordon Banks have on South African soccer that Kaizer Chiefs' longest-serving goalkeeper, Joseph 'Banks' Setlhodi, was nicknamed after him. Roger Hunt (referred to by Liverpool fans as 'Sir Roger') was regarded as one of Liverpool's greatest ever players. He was a member of the England team that won the 1966 FIFA World Cup, where he scored three times, becoming the only player ever to score a hat trick in a World Cup final. Francis Lee held the English record for the greatest number of penalties scored in a season. In 2010, he was inducted into the English Football Hall of Fame. Bobby Moore was regarded as one of the greatest defenders in the history of soccer and was the captain of the 1966 World Cup team. George Best was a skilful Irish dribbler who spent most of his footballing career at Manchester United. He was named European Footballer of the Year in 1968. Bobby Charlton played all his club football at Manchester United and was also part of the 1966 World Cup team. In the same year, he also won the Ballon d'Or.

It was indeed incredible that these great players came to play in South Africa.

There was also a tradition in the NFL of importing British players of lesser quality, leading to media criticism and frustration from the fans. Sometimes entire squads were made up of foreign players. Match attendances were falling, and this led to the formation of a subcommittee in 1974 to look into the matter. The subcommittee recommended that a minimum of three South African players (meaning White South Africans) should be fielded by each team. But the damage had been done, and the number of spectators at matches continued to dwindle.

The NFL soccer bosses would have loved to sign Black South African players such as Jomo Sono, Patrick 'Ace' Ntsoelengoe and others who dazzled the crowds with their soccer wizardry, but they always had to consider the government's stance on such matters. However, there were meetings and talks behind the scenes, paving the way to racially mixed football. One of the major indications of the popularity of racially mixed football came courtesy of the 1975 Chevrolet Champion of Champions, which pitted Black and White clubs against one another. The tournament generated significant profits and was watched by substantial crowds.

In 1976, NFL bosses expressed interest in multiracial football in which White clubs could obtain the services of players from other race groups. Those running the NPSL, on the other hand, were wary of Black players being enticed to join NFL clubs, thus weakening the NPSL. Black players were threatened with possible suspension from the South African National Football Association (SANFA) – the controlling body for Black football – and the NPSL if they played for NFL clubs. In an act of intimidation, the NPSL also warned the NFL clubs to stop trying to attract their players.

The 1977 season turned out to be the NFL's last as a major football league, leaving its member clubs at a crossroads before the 1978 season. Some NFL clubs joined the expanded NPSL, while others joined the FPL and yet others remained with the barely surviving NFL.

Sundowns quit the FPL for the NPSL early in the 1978 season. In that year, many teams in the FPL threw their weight behind the NPSL. The NPSL had been reorganised into a 'nonracial' league in which White teams were allowed to field a maximum of three Black players. This also saw movements of White players to Black teams. It was the beginning of the end for both the FPL and the NFL, and resulted in an increase in the number of teams in the NPSL. Thus, the NPSL, under George Thabe, came out victorious. The demise of both the NFL and the FPL was what he had been working hard towards. He wanted the NPSL first division to become the 'Super League' in South Africa.

With the increased number of teams in the NPSL, it became even harder for Sundowns to gain promotion to the first division. The founders of the club were also becoming drained financially, and they started looking for a buyer to save the club. It was Boy Mafa who introduced Ingle Singh, one of the cofounders of the club, to his cousin, the popular Mamelodi doctor, Dr Motsiri Itsweng.

There are stories claiming that Boy Mafa was the one who bought Sundowns from Ingle Singh and company. These are not true. According to Mike Ntombela, former Sundowns captain, Boy Mafa was a Kaizer Chiefs guy. He was not an official, but in those days there were many influential people in the clubs who were not necessarily officials or directors of the clubs. According to Ntombela, 'you must know how things worked in the past; you would find a security guy being very influential in terms of how the club is run'.

In 1979, the club was bought by Dr Motsiri Itsweng, Dr Bonny Sebotsane and Joseph Nchimane 'Fish' Kekana, all from Mamelodi in Pretoria. Kekana was a popular Mamelodi businessman, socialite, and former Transvaal Black Birds and Pretoria Hotspurs midfield maestro. Dr Itsweng and Dr Sebotsane approached the law firm Maluleke, Seriti and Moseneke to facilitate the purchase of the club. The firm was run by George Maluleke (who later became a High Court judge), Willie Seriti (who also later became a judge), and Dikgang Moseneke (who later became Deputy Chief Justice).

The new owners of Sundowns moved the team to Mamelodi, with their new home being the HM Pitje Stadium. The club then became known as Mamelodi Sundowns. They assembled a formidable squad comprising mainly students from Mamelodi High and Vlakfontein Technical, who competed strongly for league honours. They also had players such as Alpheus 'Go' Mabusela, Walter 'Mastermind' Kutumela, Andries 'Panyaza' Chitja and other high-profile players.

When Dr Itsweng and company bought the club it did not have a logo or a slogan, and they wanted to create their own identity. Someone came up with the slogan 'The sky is the limit' and they liked it. They then approached an artist and former teacher, Alexander Kenilworth Selepe, to design the logo, and the one he came up with is pretty much the same logo that is still used today.

* * *

In 1983, Sundowns gained promotion to the first division of the NPSL after a memorable match against Vaal United at HM Pitje Stadium in Pretoria. To go through, Sundowns had the tricky task of beating Vaal United by a four-goal margin. It was more of a wish than an expectation for many fans, but to everyone's delight, Sundowns were equal to the task. When Andries Chitja scored that fourth goal from the centre line, the fans went into rapture. People in Mamelodi did not sleep that Sunday, as the celebrations and jubilations continued late into the night.

After their promotion, big teams such as Kaizer Chiefs, Orlando Pirates, Moroka Swallows and others in the first division took their turn playing Sundowns on their home turf. Chiefs and Pirates had fans everywhere, including Mamelodi, and their games drew huge crowds. On match days, the streets leading to the stadium would come alive with fans clad in the colours of their favourite clubs and women selling food and drinks along the streets. There would be a carnival atmosphere in Mamelodi. This was the time when Mamelodi Sundowns truly became engraved in the hearts and minds of Mamelodi locals.

But their road in top-flight football was bumpy. They finished in fifteenth position in their inaugural year, avoiding relegation by a mere two points. The following year was hardly any better, and saw them taking fourteenth place. Things were not looking good for them, and this was draining the owners financially. Dr Itsweng and his partners were running the club mostly out of their own pockets, with a monthly bill of around R30 000.

But they were not the only ones facing tough times. Trouble was brewing in the NPSL, and things were about to explode. In January 1985, fifteen of the sixteen NPSL clubs and 30 of the second-division clubs signed a petition for George Thabe to resign. This move was instigated by a group of powerful officials led by Kaizer Motaung, Abdul Bhamjee and Cyril Kobus (the NPSL's general manager). Irvin Khoza, though not with Orlando Pirates at the time, was also working behind the scenes to get Thabe to resign. Thabe had grown too powerful and was given to making major decisions without much consultation. In particular, there was dissatisfaction with the allocation of money generated by the NPSL clubs.

The final blow came courtesy of a testimonial match for Ace Ntsoelengoe and Jomo Sono. Clubs complained that it was unfair that ten per cent of the revenue from the match was expected to go to various administrative bodies, including SANFA. Several clubs also questioned whether it wasn't a conflict of interest for Thabe to be both the chairman of the NPSL and the president of SANFA. Interestingly, Khoza was later to occupy simultaneously the positions of chairman of Orlando Pirates, chairman of the Premier Soccer League, and vice president of SAFA, resulting in the very same conflict of interest that he and the others were now accusing Thabe of having.

It was Kaizer Motaung who called for Thabe to resign. On 29 January, Thabe told those clubs wanting him to resign that he was staying put, and that they were free to break away from the NPSL if they so wished.

In the meantime, the wheels were already in motion for the breakaway group, and they were rapidly concluding sponsorship deals and securing rights to use soccer venues. South African Breweries, which had up to that point backed the NPSL, turned against it and announced that it would be backing the newly formed league with a record sponsorship of R400 000. On 19 February, the newly created National Soccer League (NSL) was formally constituted with the Castle League, made up of eighteen clubs. The NSL had essentially the same league structure as the NPSL but new management, with Thabe out of the picture. The national broadcaster, SABC TV, also signed a further R450 000 deal with the NSL for the league's broadcasting rights. They were well on their way. Leepile Taunyane became the first chairman of the NSL.

The split brought with it bitter infighting among clubs, which led to finger-pointing, stabbings, and even shootings. Rebellious players who wanted to remain with Thabe in the NPSL formed their own teams, modelled on their former teams. This led to the formation of 'The Birds' (Moroka Swallows), 'Ace Mates' (Kaizer Chiefs), and a breakaway faction of Orlando Pirates. Kaizer Chiefs midfielder Ace Ntoesolengoe and a few of his teammates, including long-serving midfield partner Jan 'Malombo' Lechaba, were responsible for the formation of Ace Mates.

The infighting in the Orlando Pirates camp led to the stabbing of a Pirates official, China 'Dibaba' Hlongwane, on 23 March 1985 in front of fans and on live TV. It was the start of the 1985 NSL Castle League Championship, and Orlando Pirates was to face Jomo Cosmos at Ellis Park Stadium. On that day, two sets of players wearing the Orlando Pirates jersey and each claiming to be the 'real' Orlando Pirates walked out onto the pitch. Hlongwane was the leader of one of the factions. To the spectators' shock, a group of men pounced on him in the centre of the field and stabbed him several times in full view of everyone. Hlongwane fought back and survived the attack – a miracle. He had been stabbed mostly in the neck and shoulders and his shirt was soaked with blood. But he was still standing. He was rushed to hospital and the match with the real Pirates went on. It ended in a 2–2 draw.

'I am not the dying type,' Hlongwane said afterwards in an interview. But his luck ran out just a few years later, when he was shot dead by an unknown gunman.

The day before the infamous stabbing at Ellis Park, a Moroka Swallows defender, Aaron 'Roadblock' Makhathini, was gunned down outside his Pimville home while returning from training. Makhathini and other Swallows players, including Aubrey 'The Great' Makgopela, Frederick 'Congo' Malebane, Joe 'Ace' Mnini, and Samuel 'Happy Cow' Nkomo had formed their own team,

The Birds. Two Swallows officials, James Ngidi and club chairman David 'Pine' Chabeli, were arrested but later discharged. No charges were brought against them. Everybody knew that it was because of the split that Makhathini had been gunned down, but there was no evidence pointing directly at the two officials. Soccer in those days was such an emotional affair that fans sometimes took matters into their own hands. Could it have been one of those highly emotional fans? Not enough investigation went into it, and Makhathini's death became another 'shot dead by an unknown gunman' case.

The league needed stabilising and the bloodshed needed to stop. Stability finally returned when it became evident to those who had been refusing to leave the NPSL that they were fighting a losing battle. Orlando Pirates stabilised and so did Moroka Swallows and Kaizer Chiefs. There was no saving the NPSL from its demise.

* * *

Mamelodi Sundowns continued to find the going tough in the newly formed NSL. Towards the end of the season, they were hovering in the drop zone, with only eleven more games to play. They had never won a game and the only points they had collected – ten, to be exact – were from drawn games. The dream of keeping Mamelodi Sundowns in top-flight football was slowly dying, and the possibility of the franchise leaving Mamelodi – should they decide to sell the club – loomed large. There was even the threat of the team being disbanded if they did not find a buyer. They were looking for a buyer who would keep the dream alive for Mamelodi people.

This was when the flamboyant Mahobe came waltzing in with a briefcase full of money. He went with Snowy and a friend of his, Jabu 'Nyambose' Mthethwa, to negotiate the purchase of the club. Mthethwa was a well-known businessman from Senaoane, Soweto, and a very close friend of Mahobe's.

Mthethwa was one of the team's senior officials, even though he had no official position. As part of Mahobe's inner circle, he had a big influence on what went on. If anybody needed money and Mahobe was not there, they would go to him and he would treat them the same way that Mahobe would. Players and team officials trusted him.

It was Mthethwa who persuaded Mike Ntombela to join Sundowns. 'In 1985 I was playing for Wits University FC but was looking for a move to another club,' explained Ntombela. 'My friend, Mike Mangena, who I had played with at Wits, had just moved to Durban Bush Bucks for a fee of R27 000.'

Ntombela used to go to the city library in town to study, as he was doing a degree with UNISA, and during lunchtime there were often a lot of people there at the library grounds. 'We used to see a lot of famous people, like Dancing Shoes Morake, the famous boxer, who used to work nearby to the library. One of the people that I met there was Screamer Tshabalala, who was with the late Coloured Passmore, owner of Alexandra township-based Giant Blackpool FC, where Screamer was coaching. And he told me there was this guy called Zola Mahobe who had money, and he was looking for me.'

Ntombela realised it wasn't by coincidence that he had met Screamer there – they must have been following him, as it wasn't the first time that Sundowns had approached him. In 1984, Fish

Kekana, one of the owners of Mamelodi Sundowns, and Joe Matimba, who was a security guy, had invited him to come to Pretoria to watch a Sundowns game. He had gone to the game and liked what he saw. But he had made no commitment to moving. And now here they were again.

'I listened to Screamer but played hard to get, and the conversation ended there. Besides, I didn't know who this Mahobe was in soccer. He was an unknown. I was sceptical.'

Screamer was friends with Mahobe. Even though he was still coaching Giant Blackpool, he was already recruiting players for Sundowns. He had a way of quickly becoming friends with his bosses.

When the season finished, Ntombela was ready to make a move, but none of the big teams like Kaizer Chiefs, Pirates, or Swallows was interested in him. Then one Sunday, while he was selling vegetables at his stall, he was approached by Jabu Mthethwa, who told him that Mahobe wanted to meet with him.

'He has a lot of money and he has just bought Sundowns. He wants you to join them,' explained Mthethwa.

Ntombela was reluctant. Besides, he was not properly dressed for a meeting – he was in his work overalls. But Mthethwa was not taking no for an answer and finally convinced him. 'We are with him in Diepkloof as we speak and I want you to go there with me to meet him.'

They drove to Diepkloof, to the house of another of Mahobe's close friends, Six Morake, where Mahobe was. He was impressed with the way Mahobe looked, with his designer suit, an open shirt and a nice gold chain around his neck. Looking at him, one smelt money.

Then the negotiations started. But Ntombela still did not trust him. He doubted that he could afford him.

'How much do you want?' Mahobe asked him.

Ntombela knew that Mike Mangena was sold to Bush Bucks for R27 000. So he started playing the bargaining game. 'I want about R30 000,' he said. Not that he thought he was better than Mangena, but he was not going to sell himself cheap.

Mahobe was quiet for a while and then laughed and said, 'I can go to R35 000.'

Ntombela could not believe it. 'What about my terms?'

'You can come to my office tomorrow,' he said.

The following morning he went to the office and Mahobe was very professional. For the first time in his life, Ntombela was offered a signing-on fee. He was excited.

He then called the Wits FC boss, Professor Ronnie Schloss, and told him of his intention to leave. Schloss did not take the news well. Joe Frickleton, who was head coach, was also opposed to the move. But there was nothing they could do to stop him.

Ntombela was so excited about the move that he also started recruiting players for Sundowns. He was friends with Pitso Mosimane, who was with Cosmos at the time, and he encouraged him and Mike Mangena to join Sundowns. As he explained, 'Zola was a big brother to me. He was a boss, a mentor. He bought a club in Mamelodi and kept it there. Not many people could do that. He made me love Mamelodi. First, it was Fish Kekana; second, it was Joe Matimba; third, it was Zola Mahobe; fourth, it was the people of Mamelodi – they welcomed us with open arms.'

He was right about Mahobe keeping the club in Mamelodi. Normally when people from different areas bought soccer clubs, they moved them to their area. Jomo Sono had done that with

Cosmos. But in this case, Mahobe was the one doing the travelling from Soweto to Mamelodi. This was, in part, because of the terms set by Dr Itsweng, Dr Sebotsane and Fish Kekana – who remained directors of the team – that the team should not be relocated from Mamelodi. But Mahobe, being the majority shareholder, could have relocated the club if he had so wished.

* * *

Mahobe was ready to make his move. He is reported to have offered the owners of Sundowns R100 000 for an 80% stake in the club – an offer that was too good to be refused. And so, at the age of 31, Zola Mahobe stepped into a new identity as the owner of a football team. The purchase was facilitated by the law firm Maluleke, Seriti and Moseneke, which Mahobe retained as the club's legal counsel.

He then appointed Ben Segale, who had coached him during his soccer-playing years, as the team coach and introduced huge financial incentives for the players. Segale, who had also previously coached Orlando Pirates, was at the time coaching Mmabatho Kicks FC in Bophuthatswana (now part of North West). The result of these changes was that Sundowns won their next ten matches and drew the last, ending the season in eleventh position, with 31 points. (In those days, a win was worth two points and not three, as is the case in modern football.)

Mahobe was declaring to all and sundry that money was not an issue. He was hungry to take his place among the 'top dogs' of soccer. The disappointment of not being able to lay his hands on Orlando Pirates was a faded memory, replaced by the exciting challenge of turning Sundowns around and sending them shooting to the top of the NSL. The headquarters of the team was also on Eloff Street, on the same floor as Power Promotions, so he could manage all his businesses from a central location.

Mahobe then went on a spending spree to recruit players. In January 1986 he paid a record fee of R40 000 for striker Mike 'Sporo' Mangena of 1985 NSL champions Bush Bucks FC and formerly of Watford FC and Kaizer Chiefs, which was a record for a local player. Before mid-season he paid another R40 000 for 'Big John' Salter from neighbours Arcadia FC. Then he brought Pitso Mosimane in from Jomo Cosmos, for a new record fee of R60 000. But it didn't stop there – he signed up players like Andries 'Panyaza' Chitja, Mark 'Lesilo' Anderson, Bricks Mudau, Harold 'Jazzy Queen' Legodi, and Lovemore Chafunya. In less than two years he had spent over R2 million on the club – by far the biggest expenditure by any club boss on a team at the time. Sundowns was turning into a beast.

Despite all these records, the biggest money yet spent in Black South African soccer belonged to a Brazilian player, Jair Ventura Filho, better known as Jairzinho. A quick, powerful winger, he had been a member of the Brazilian national team that won the 1970 FIFA World Cup, during which he scored in every game that Brazil played and earned himself the nickname 'The Hurricane'. He was listed as number 27 in the *World Soccer* magazine's list of the 100 greatest players of the 20th century, one place ahead of Zinedine Zidane. Jairzinho, a former Botafogo player, was invited by Ewert Nene, one of the cofounders of Kaizer Chiefs, to come and play a few games for Kaizer Chiefs in 1975, during the Brazil off-season. Chiefs paid a record fee of R70 000 for him. He left a lasting impression on South African fans by scoring seven goals in the three matches that he played for Chiefs.

***

The final piece of the puzzle at Sundowns was a coach who would match the fashionable new image of the club, and Mahobe turned to the charismatic Stanley 'Screamer' Tshabalala, who was at the time working for Blackpool FC. In his playing days, Tshabalala used to mesmerise the crowds with his amazing football skills – sometimes standing on top of the ball just to show off – and his incessant screaming for the ball. Fans always waited keenly for him to turn on the style and live up to his Screamer nickname.

Mahobe came looking for him when he was still coaching for Blackpool. He offered him R50 000 – a lot of money back then – to leave Blackpool. After Mahobe had shared his vision with him, he did not hesitate to accept the offer to coach Sundowns. Mahobe was elated.

Mahobe was happiest when Sundowns beat Kaizer Chiefs, partly because of his childhood love for Orlando Pirates. The Chiefs had given Pirates trouble right from the beginning, so it was sweet revenge to see them getting a dose of their own medicine. Also, Mamelodi Sundowns was the new kid on the block, while Chiefs was one of the big boys, so beating them was the type of surprise that drove the fans wild.

It was clear that Mahobe's master plan was working – he was taking the fight to the big guys. In no time at all he'd taken a mediocre local team, supercharged it with high-octane players and high-flying ambition, and made it one of the most famous teams in the first division. His achievements have been likened to those of Manchester City's Abu Dhabi owners, who propelled the club into the European elite in just a few short years through grand ambitions matched by vast spending.

According to Tshabalala, all he had to do was point and say, 'I need this player,' and Mahobe would get the player for him. If anyone had financial troubles, Mahobe would be the generous father who came along and made everything right. Nobody knew where the money was coming from, but they were prepared to ignore their doubts and enjoy the sunshine while it lasted.

Mahobe didn't just bring a culture of big spending to local soccer, he also brought a spirit of real professionalism. This is something that is easy to overlook if one focuses only on the dubious sources of his wealth. For the first time in the history of the NSL and its predecessors, he turned players into full-time professionals and had them sign actual contracts. It was a trend that the rest of the clubs would soon follow. He also provided the team with professional training facilities, introduced a better salary system, and offered better incentives. He brought on board a technical sponsor, Kappa, who was also the technical sponsor for Kaizer Chiefs. He made the players understand the importance of playing good, winning football, and the club routinely attracted crowds of over 20 000.

Mamelodi Sundowns attracted supporters away from Chiefs, Pirates and Swallows. People threw away their other memberships in favour of Sundowns. The club also had a strong following in Bloemfontein and Durban. Mahobe's squad was the envy of many a soccer boss. It was also the dream of many players to play for Sundowns. The money was good, the mood was good, and Zola Mahobe and Sundowns were the talk of the town. What more could they wish for?

* * *

Having bought the country's top talent, Mahobe set about turning his players into media stars. Before he took over Mamelodi Sundowns, only players from Orlando Pirates, Kaizer Chiefs and Moroka Swallows were household names in Soweto. It was not a difficult task thrusting his players into the limelight, however, as he had big-name players and the club was winning games. The media also loved him, and he made sure there was always something new at Sundowns or in his personal life to keep their appetites whetted. He was also the first soccer boss to have a club magazine: *The Mamelodi Sundowns Magazine*. He went out of his way to register supporters for the club, both in Soweto and in many other parts of the country. It was part of his grand plan to turn Mamelodi Sundowns into a leading brand in South Africa. Needless to say, other clubs followed suit.

Let everybody be happy, then the money will flow in. Mahobe doted on his players and staff, showering them with expensive gifts, including top-of-the-range BMWs and even houses. There was also a lot of partying in Pretoria, each time Sundowns played at home.

'Ag man ... that guy was a good guy,' one of his friends, Ace, from Rockville, Soweto, once said. 'We used to have nice times with that guy. Whether Sundowns won or lost, it didn't matter; we would all go to Pretoria and have a good party.' He loved splashing out on food and beverages. He bought booze for his friends and guests, but he never drank with them, nor was he ever seen drinking in public. He could tolerate one or two glasses of bubbly, though, on special occasions. He also never talked much about himself; not about his upbringing in Soweto and not about his business path.

In his memoir, *My Own Liberator*, Dikgang Moseneke tells the story of how Mahobe often invited him and Willie Seriti to Mamelodi Sundowns games. He provided them with business class tickets and hotel accommodation, and when he was happy (which was most of the time) he liked saying to them, 'I am a man of many challenges. I like to travel with my lawyers and my gunman next to me.' They were concerned about the bit equating lawyers with gunmen – there was a Mafia ring to it. They were right; it was the Mafia gangs who equated lawyers with gunmen. To the Mafia, these people were mere protectors and facilitators – they protected them from harm and from the law, and they facilitated business, which often involved eliminating those who stood in the way. Mahobe listened attentively when they talked, which was one of the traits of big gangsters. He had also paid for the purchase of Sundowns in cash, which made his sources of income questionable. His spending just seemed to have no boundaries, which raised questions about exactly how much money he had. Where was he getting it from? Could it be true that he needed his gunman next to him? They were justified in being concerned. But it was just Mahobe covering his tracks and diverting attention away from his true sources of income. He dared not let anyone even get a whiff of it.

* * *

Despite his love for Sundowns and his dedication to the club, Mahobe's fondness for Orlando Pirates would always stay with him. Even though he had his own team and was competing for the same glory as Pirates, he never turned his back on them. He was still their godfather and still wanted them to win trophies. He was especially concerned when Orlando Pirates started struggling and began to be threatened with relegation. He lent them players, saying he wanted to help them in their fight against relegation. That year, Orlando Pirates finished fifteenth, with 24 points, just two points above bottom-of-the-log Cape Town Spurs and one point above Benoni United and African Wanderers. They also won the fewest games – five, to be exact – and had a miserable goal difference of minus nineteen. Despite this dismal performance, Mahobe could sit back with satisfaction, knowing he had helped them avoid relegation.

* * *

There were always movements of players at Sundowns, as the officials tried to find the perfect combinations for their style of football. Hardly a month went by without the excitement of yet another Mahobe signing or something interesting happening in the Mamelodi Sundowns camp. He wasn't afraid to let players go, even if he'd paid a lot for them. He let Andries Chitja go to Moroka Swallows. And when he tired of his other pricey signing, Mike Mangena, he swapped him with Swallows to get Chitja back. Mangena had been with the team barely five months, having signed on in January 1986 and being sold to Swallows in June. John Salter, another high-ticket signing, went back to Arcadia after just two months, in exchange for flying fullback Trevor Klein.

To some, all this chopping and changing might have seemed chaotic, but Mahobe was working to a plan. His vision for Sundowns was to build a team that would compete with the best in the world. The sky was the limit, as those who had coined the Sundowns slogan had prophesied correctly. He especially liked the way the Brazilian team played, and he nicknamed Mamelodi Sundowns 'The Brazilians'. He even picked Brazilian national soccer team colours for Sundowns.

In Mahobe's book, Italian soccer was also up there in the same league as that of Brazil. Italy had won the FIFA World Cup in 1982 – the third time since the inception of the tournament. There were also exciting players in Serie A, such as Roberto Donadoni, who had a blistering pace down the right-hand side that pulled defences apart and created chances for goals for his teammates. Other stars included Michel Platini, who won three consecutive Ballon d'Or awards, Diego Maradona, arguably one of the two most talented men ever to play the game, and Roberto Baggio, a set-piece specialist known for pace, technique and uncanny vision.

Mahobe arranged for Tshabalala to go to Italy for coaching clinics, to hone his coaching skills. The Casaletti family of Rob, Emmy and Vivian – the owners of Kappa – were the ones who took him there. In Italy, he visited AC Milan and Juventus. It was after coming home from Italy that Tshabalala coined the phrase 'shoeshine and piano' to describe the style of soccer that Mamelodi Sundowns should play. What did it mean?

As the story goes, when Tshabalala was in Italy, the Italian coach who was working with him kept on shouting words in Italian that sounded like 'Piano! Piano! Shoeshine! Piano!' When he asked for the interpretation of 'piano' he was told that it meant 'easy'. The concept, according to Trott Moloto, meant building up play from the back, neatly passing through tight spaces, and keeping things calm while dominating the opponent.

'Shoeshine and piano' was the perfect description of the Sundowns style – polished, perfectly tuned, and artfully played. After all, Sundowns was a fashionable and stylish team, hence their other nickname, *Bafana ba style*, the stylish boys.

Tshabalala also encouraged his players to learn about soccer as much as they could through the media. Thus, they frequented Karos Hotel in Hillbrow, which was popular among hip and happening Black people in those days, especially soccer players.

According to Ntombela, Hillbrow became a popular winding-down place for dedicated footballers, where they bought overseas football magazines and newspapers or watched games at the hotel in an effort to sharpen their skills. Footballers were hungry for knowledge, to improve their understanding of the game, and they took fitness very seriously. 'Screamer influenced a lot of us to visit these areas during our off days,' says Ntombela. 'I used to go there with Pitso Mosimane, Harold Legodi, Ace Khuse, and Rabbi Moripe, just to mention a few.'

* * *

Mahobe also never hesitated to ruffle feathers. After swapping Mike Mangena to get Andries Chitja back from Swallows, he went to court to have him cleared to play in the 1986 Mainstay Cup. He won the case and Chitja played in the tournament, even scoring a goal against Kaizer Chiefs in the quarter-final.

He also challenged the NSL administration over the allocation of gate receipts, calling a media conference to announce an official rebellion. But in the end, he proved unequal to the task of changing things he thought were wrong. He was relatively new to soccer administration and naive about many behind-the-scenes matters in soccer, but he did get the NSL administration worried. He and the NSL officials called a truce in early 1987.

Mahobe also petitioned the Northern Transvaal Rugby Union (NTRU) and the Pretoria City Council to allow the giant Loftus Versfeld Stadium to be used as an alternative home ground for Mamelodi Sundowns, especially for crowd-pulling games like those against Kaizer Chiefs, Moroka Swallows, and Orlando Pirates. But the NTRU and Pretoria City Council were not willing. 'They are hiding behind excuses,' said the then Sundowns public relations officer (PRO), Ngamula Malewa. 'At first, the excuse was that they had not received our application. We hand-delivered the application and expected to be invited for talks, but next thing we hear through the press that our application has been turned down. I still maintain that the NTRU and the City Council should have been decent enough to inform us by letter that our plans had fallen through.'

Mahobe and his Sundowns had the support of the NSL PRO, Abdul Bhamjee, who was adamant that the decision was an act of racism. 'I am totally disgusted,' said the furious Bhamjee. 'When, in this so-called enlightened period, will they wake up?'

But Mahobe's efforts were not in vain, as in years to come, soccer was allowed at Loftus Versfeld, and the stadium did become an alternative home ground for Mamelodi Sundowns.

Abdul Bhamjee has been described by Billy Cooper of *City Press* as 'the original razzmatazz' who 'could sell ice to an Inuit'. Others called him 'Mr Soccer'. His title as PRO of the NPSL and later the NSL concealed the power that he had. Apart from being at the forefront of the formation of the NSL, he was also the driving force behind the building of the original FNB Stadium.

As a PRO, he was a sports journalist's dream, and fans always looked forward to his interviews. When he talked, the whole soccer world listened. He always knew what to say to keep the fans hooked on soccer, and he packed stadiums. Bhamjee was also one of the forces behind nonracialism in soccer, and he was the driving force behind negotiations for soccer to be played at the Ellis Park rugby stadium. No one who was at the Ellis Park Stadium the day it was opened for soccer will forget how the stadium, which had a capacity of 67 000, was crammed almost to the touchline with 100 000 spectators. Bhamjee, like the conductor of a massive orchestra, went around the pitch moving the spectators who were sitting too close to the line. He was loved and admired by the soccer fraternity. There has been no PRO like Bhamjee since in South African soccer.

His fall from grace came in 1991, when he was convicted of fraud relating to R7 million in NSL sponsorship money. He proclaimed his innocence, insisting that he was entitled to the money, but the courts were having none of it. He was sentenced to a fourteen-year jail term, but was released on parole in July 1996 after serving just over four years of the term. This prematurely ended his career in soccer. He died in 2021, aged 82.

* * *

Mahobe was enjoying the fruits of his labour at Sundowns. Under coach Screamer Tshabalala the 'shoeshine and piano' style became the popular style in town, as Mahobe and Sundowns made it clear that they were not just there in the NSL to add numbers. Everybody was talking about them. In the next two years, they were an all-conquering side, winning almost everything and ending the monopoly of the Soweto big three – Orlando Pirates, Kaizer Chiefs and Moroka Swallows. From 1986 to 1988 they won the Mainstay Cup, the BP Top 8, the Olsson's Challenge Cup, and the NSL Castle League Championship.

Mahobe's sweetest moment was when they won the Mainstay Cup in 1986, as this was the first trophy for Sundowns. In the quarter-finals, they beat Kaizer Chiefs 3–2 at Orlando Stadium under controversial circumstances. Chiefs' goals were scored by Abel Shongwe and Chippa Molatedi (penalty), and Sundowns' goals by Andries Chitja, Lovemore Chafunya and Pitso Mosimane (penalty).

Kaizer Chiefs was always the team to beat. In 1984, they won the Castle League, Mainstay Cup, JPS Knockout, and Sales House trophies. And in 1985, they won the Champion of Champions and BP Top 8 trophies. They were always there, always competing for top honours.

As the good results came rolling in, the players, technical staff and officials received pleasantly surprising news from Mahobe: he promised them an all-expenses-paid trip to the 1986 FA Cup Final in London. They were even more surprised when he announced that their partners were also invited.

Sundowns beat Moroka Swallows 3–2 in the semi-final of the Mainstay Cup, but their win against Chiefs was that much sweeter. Mahobe's dream was about to be realised. Sundowns met Jomo Cosmos in the final at Ellis Park Stadium on Sunday, 3 December 1986, in front of a capacity crowd. The Sundowns starting eleven consisted of Mark Anderson, Vincent Makroti, Sam 'Eewie' Kambule, Johannes 'Bricks' Mudau, William Zondi, Jan 'Malombo' Lechaba, Andries Chitja, Pitso 'Jingles' Mosimane, Rabbi Moripe, Lovemore Chafunya, and Ace Khuse. They were outplayed, but deep into extra time a Sundowns player crossed the ball into the box, hoping to find his teammates, but they were nowhere to be seen. Instead, two Cosmos players, one of them Greg Cupido, chased after the ball, as their goalkeeper also went out of his box to intercept it. The goalkeeper and Cupido got to the ball together, with no pressure at all from the Sundowns players, who were metres away. As the goalkeeper tried to collect the ball, Cupido was trying to clear it for a corner, and they clashed. Cupido lost his balance and the ball went into his net. Sundowns won the match 1–0.

This victory was the big break Sundowns and Mahobe had been working for – suddenly they were no longer just a small-town team, but were up there with the stars. The fans loved them and the whole country celebrated. Drinks at taverns and shebeens in Mamelodi went at half-price, and people did not sleep that night, as they celebrated until the early hours. It was a proud day – the first time that a major trophy had come to Mamelodi.

The formal prize-giving ceremony was held in Johannesburg the following Wednesday. Sundowns were presented with their trophy and medals, as well as prize money of R50 000. Cosmos received R25 000, while semi-finalists Moroka Swallows and Orlando Pirates each collected R12 000.

On the day of the 'people's celebrations' there was a carnival atmosphere in Mamelodi. Mahobe had hired a number of classic American convertibles – the ones made popular by the Americans gang of Sophiatown and similar gangs that followed – and an open double-decker bus for the players. The parade started in the city of Pretoria and made its way slowly to Mamelodi, with the players waving their trophy and receiving the cheers of their fans all the way. The parade went slowly through the streets of Mamelodi, which were lined with fans clad in their yellow and green T-shirts and waving flags, posters and banners. The procession ended at HM Pitje stadium. It was the biggest celebration the people of Mamelodi had ever seen – a celebration fit for a king and his knights. Cattle were slaughtered and there was meat and pap and *umqombothi*. Mahobe had also roped in South African Breweries, who were eager sponsors of soccer, to provide free beer.

The following weekend there was a small parade in Johannesburg – nothing like the scale of the one in Mamelodi. It was more like a wedding procession through the city. The parade ended at the Carlton Hotel, where the celebrations were to take place. This was in keeping with Mahobe's style. The Carlton Hotel was popular with the rich and famous. Henry Kissinger, Francois Mitterand, Hillary Clinton, Margaret Thatcher, Whitney Houston and Mick Jagger were among the hotel's guests during its 25-year history.

Money can't buy loyalty
– *Sofa silahlane*

Despite Mahobe's fat chequebook, there were some players his money could not buy. One such player was Nelson 'Teenage' Dladla, a tricky Kaizer Chiefs winger who was making a nuisance of himself against opposing teams. He was a dribbling wizard and was almost unstoppable, weaving between the opposition and twisting and turning like a gazelle being chased by a cheetah.

Dladla was from the small town of Springs, where he had started out playing for a team called Pilkington Young Brothers FC. Word in the soccer circles has it that when Mahobe announced that he was interested in buying Dladla, Kaizer Chiefs put a ridiculously high price tag of R500 000 on their most prized asset, convinced it would scare Mahobe off. It was more than the price of a whole franchise in the same division at the time. It was only when Mahobe came striding into the Kaizer Chiefs offices with a big briefcase full of cash that Chiefs insisted that their star left-winger was not for sale – at any price.

Teenage Dladla was synonymous with Kaizer Chiefs and was a crowd favourite. Selling him would have been bound to cause an upset and even a riot. Yes, people jumped up and down with joy and forgot their political and financial woes at the stadiums, but soccer was more than mere entertainment – it was a religion. Families would stop talking to each other or even fight with each other because of opposing club loyalties or lost matches. Fights would also break out at the stadiums and in the streets among opposing fans, usually started by those of the losing team.

Dladla had been worth his weight in gold, even before he made it to Amakhosi, and some people would go to any lengths to keep him. When the Amakhosi bosses had set their sights on the youngster, they sent Ewert Nene, the greatest soccer marketer of the time, to recruit him. On 10 August 1976, Nene went to the Dladla household in KwaThema, a township south-west of Springs, to negotiate his transfer. He was supposed to have gone with Kaizer Motaung, but Motaung was not ready to leave by the time Ewert got to his house. Ewert was in a hurry because he also wanted to see some people while he was there, so he decided to go with Jan 'Malombo' Lechaba instead.

The transfer negotiations were successful, and Nene crammed Dladla into the back seat of his Chevrolet Impala and covered him with a blanket so he would not be recognised. But word of Dladla's defection had already spread, and a mob was waiting for the car as it drove away. They stopped the car and demanded that Nene leave their star player with them. He refused, tempers raged, and a man stepped forward and stabbed Nene to death. Dladla went on to play for Chiefs and repaid Nene's faith in him with years of loyal service to the club.

Another player Mahobe's money could not buy was Johnny 'Black Sunday' Masegela – a formidable striker playing for Jomo Cosmos. Masegela got his nickname after scoring four goals on a Sunday for Jomo Cosmos against Orlando Pirates. Masegela says that Mahobe approached him one day, in the presence of Cosmos owner Jomo Sono, and said he wanted him for Sundowns. 'Just tell me you will play for Sundowns and the deal is done,' said Mahobe. 'Don't worry about this one [referring to Sono]; he likes money. I'll just give him money and he won't say no.'

It was an awkward moment for both Sono and Masegela. 'Jomo hated Mahobe's guts,' said Masegela. 'Mahobe had already taken Pitso Mosimane away from him for a record fee of R60 000. But I didn't want to be seen to be choosing money over loyalty, so I stayed at Cosmos. Besides, we were playing good soccer at the time. We ended fourth on the NSL log that year, while Sundowns ended eleventh.' When Masegela eventually left Cosmos, he signed up with Orlando Pirates.

The relationship between Mahobe and Sono cannot be said to have been a good one. There was some arrogance in Mahobe towards Sono. Motaung, Sono and Mahobe were the three Soweto boys on everyone's lips at that time – the great soccer bosses. Mahobe wanted to be the *'makhulu baas'* (the big boss), and it was Kaizer Chiefs that he wanted to outdo, not Jomo Cosmos. Cosmos did not have the glamour of Kaizer Chiefs and Mamelodi Sundowns. That was another reason why the win against Chiefs was that much sweeter to him.

* * *

Mahobe was also after the signature of Isaac 'Shakes' Kungwane. Kungwane had been spotted by the Kaizer Chiefs head of development, Vincent Williams. But two other teams, Orlando Pirates and Mamelodi Sundowns, were also after his signature. In his typical style, Mahobe went to Kungwane's home with a briefcase full of money to lure him to Sundowns. Even though what Mahobe put on the table financially was more than Chiefs or Pirates could afford, Kungwane turned him down. However, it was difficult for him to say no to Pirates, as he had grown up a Pirates fan. It was Teenage Dladla who played a major role in persuading him to join Chiefs. He promised to give him his number 11 jersey. It was a touching gesture for a player of Teenager's calibre to promise him his jersey. Jersey number 11 has always been a special jersey at Kaizer Chiefs. Apart from Dladla and Kungwane, it has been worn by legends like Emmanuel 'Scara' Ngobese, Jabu Pule (Mahlangu) and Knowledge Musona.

Kungwane was a goal assister extraordinaire. His job, as he put it, was 'to create goals and spoon-feed players' like Fani Madida, Shane McGregor and Pollen (Ndlanya). His wizardry and precise passing earned him the respect of his teammates and the opposition alike.

There were other players Mahobe's money could not buy, not because they were earning more money at their clubs than what he was offering, but because of loyalty and the fact that their clubs were not willing to part with them at any price. This was good for competition, because it meant that money wasn't everything. Which team could have competed with Sundowns if Mahobe had managed to get every player he wanted?

Mother of all parties
– Ngisho abelungu abakhoni

Mahobe decided to fulfil his promise of taking the team to London to watch the FA Cup Final. The English Premier League was the most popular overseas league in South Africa, in part because many of England's victorious 1966 FIFA World Cup players had played in South Africa in the 1970s.

'Your partners are also invited,' declared Mahobe. 'Whether she's your girlfriend or your wife, it doesn't matter; we're going to London!' He also told them to pack their boots, as he had a few practice matches lined up for them.

'Hey, guys, the big man is serious; he's really taking us to London,' players started murmuring among themselves.

Preparations for the trip started in earnest and visa applications were processed. It was now clear that Mahobe's spending could not have been sustained by his businesses. He had to have another source of income that nobody knew about. But who cared? Sundowns was living in the world of milk and honey. No team boss had ever done anything like this. Most of the players had never travelled outside the country. They were the envy of all their acquaintances and of many other soccer players. Travelling to London was a big deal. Girls wished they had a Sundowns player or official for a boyfriend. Not everyone took a partner, not because they were not allowed to, but because they chose not to. The number of people going on the trip came to 53. Gladys and Stix were among them.

News of the trip to London set tongues wagging. Mahobe was feted by the media, and everybody was in awe of the fact that the invitation had been extended to the players' and officials' partners. It was official – Zola Mahobe was the richest Black man in South Africa. No Black tycoon could spend money like that, not even Richard Maponya, who was perhaps the most well-known Soweto tycoon before Mahobe. A teacher by training, Maponya had started out as an employee of a clothing company, where he was a salesman, selling clothes to miners and rural people. He excelled at the job and his White bosses were impressed. But they could not promote him to the position of general manager because then he would have had to oversee White employees. As a consolation, they gave him cloth samples and imperfect clothing, which he sold in his spare time. This allowed him to build up his own capital. When his patron retired in 1956, his supply of stock stopped. He left the company and tried to open his own clothing retail business, but was denied a licence. They did give him a licence to sell food, however, and this became the kernel of his fortune. He set up the Dube Hygienic Dairy, which delivered milk to people without electricity or refrigerators. He went on to open a butchery, two grocery stores, a restaurant, a filling station, a General Motors dealership, bottle stores, a bus transport business, and a successful BMW dealership in Soweto. He later became the chairperson of Kilimanjaro Holdings, a bottling company which was formed after Coca-Cola decided to disinvest in South Africa.

Despite all this, Maponya did not have money to spend the way Mahobe did – and he worked hard for it. He was a man focused on building his empire and only managed to spend a little here and there on charitable endeavours, whereas Mahobe was more focused on spending money. Mahobe's wealth was not counted in terms of assets, but based on how much he had to spend. Nobody else had money to spend so freely.

* * *

One of the main reasons the English Premier League held such a special place in the hearts of South Africans was that, in those days, it was the only regular international football that South Africans could watch on TV. Even though apartheid state television prioritised the sporting tastes of Whites by giving preference to sports such as rugby and cricket, it also broadcast highlights of the English First Division on the BBC's famous *Match of the Day* programme, presented by the legendary Jimmy Hill. It was like magic, watching those players play. It was a world that many Black South African players yearned to be in. The English Premier League also had great players from all over the world, including Black players such as Paul Canoville of Chelsea, Howard Gayle of Sunderland, and Laurie Cunningham – a Leicester City and former Real Madrid player.

The bond between Black South African soccer and English soccer was formed back in 1955, when Stephen Madi Mokone, the former Durban Bush Bucks player fondly known as 'Kalamazoo' or 'Black Meteor', joined Coventry City in England, where he made four appearances, scoring one goal. He later played in the Netherlands for Heracles Almelo, scoring twice in his debut match and earning them the 1958 Second Division title. He signed for a few other clubs after that, including Barcelona, and ended his footballing career at Sunshine George Cross in Australia. He would go on to have a crazy life, obtaining a doctorate from an American university, becoming an assistant professor in psychiatry, and also becoming a leading light in the anti-apartheid movement. It got even crazier when he was charged with throwing acid in the face of his ex-wife – a charge he always disputed. It was later suspected that he had been framed in a collaboration between the American Central Intelligence Agency (CIA) and the apartheid government because of his pro-ANC alignment.

But it was the exceptionally talented Leeds United winger, Albert 'Hurry Hurry' Johanneson, also known as 'The Black Flash', who made a lasting impression on the English soccer scene. He first joined Leeds United in 1961 from Germiston Colliers on a three-month trial, after which Leeds decided to sign him. In the 1962/63 season, he was the second-highest scorer, with fourteen goals, and only missed one game. In the 1963/64 season he was the team's joint top scorer, with fifteen goals. His chief asset was a blinding natural pace. He also had a bag full of tricks and a good eye for goal. But it was his role as the chief entertainer in an otherwise uncolourful team that really made him the favourite with the Leeds fans.

But Johanneson had been poisoned by apartheid. It is said that at the beginning he was unsure whether he was allowed to share the communal showers with his White teammates, until one day they stripped him and threw him in. He was also reluctant when a White apprentice was asked to clean his boots. Apartheid had conditioned him that way, and it was hard for him to see himself differently. He was not the first one. In 1958, Darius Mfana Dhlomo, another Black South African player who played for Heracles Almelo, sent his teammates and officials into a panic during his debut game when he went missing, triggering a frantic search. He was found by a teammate changing underneath the grandstand, thinking that since he was Black, he was not allowed into the changing room.

Johanneson became the first Coloured South African, and the first player of colour, to feature in an FA Cup Final – the 1965 final – in a match they played against Liverpool. They lost the match 2–1 in extra time.

It was after this final that his downfall began. The whole team did not perform well, but much of the focus was on Johanneson. He was also disappointed in himself. From that point on he never seemed the same again. Was he subject to hate speech during the game? Yes, he was. Johanneson faced abuse both on the football pitch and off it. He was verbally abused and physically intimidated. Players such as George Best talked openly about it. Overcome by depression, he took to booze. As a result, he began to struggle to maintain that which had earned him the nickname 'Hurry Hurry': his fitness.

He left Leeds for York City, but the downward spiral continued until he quit football and sank into a hopeless battle with alcoholism. He died alone in his flat in Leeds in 1995, an unbelievable talent strangled by a very cruel society.

In 2019, Leeds United FC unveiled a Leeds Civic Trust Blue Plaque to honour Johanneson.

The other South African players who played for Leeds United were Philemon Masinga and Lucas 'The Chief' Radebe. Radebe went on to become captain of Leeds.

Mahobe admired Albert Johanneson. He was a living example showing that South Africa had players who could take the country to the top. 'You see, Ma-J, Ma-Six, Ma-Stix, apartheid has taken a lot from us,' he would say to Jabu Mthethwa, Six Morake and Stix, his inner circle in matters of soccer. 'That guy, Hurry Hurry, was a clear example that we are as good in soccer as anybody else in this world. We are in isolation, yes, but we can still enjoy world-class soccer. That's why it is important for our coach to be exposed to international methods of coaching and our players to get international exposure. I am not talking TV here, but the actual experience of playing against some of these overseas-based players. We will find holes in the system to get it done.' They were in agreement. Taking Sundowns to London to watch the FA Cup Final and having them play a few practice games was a small but significant step towards the top.

Another bond between Black South African soccer fans and English soccer was formed through players with a South African connection playing in England, such as Gary Bailey, Bruce Grobbelaar and Craig Johnston. Gary Bailey, although born in England, was raised in South Africa. He started his career at Wits University FC and went on to play for Manchester United. He was reserve goalkeeper on the England squad for the 1986 World Cup in Mexico, but only won two caps. Bruce Grobbelaar was born in Durban but grew up in neighbouring Rhodesia (Zimbabwe). Craig Johnston was Australian, his only South African connection being that his father had taken up a job in Johannesburg and briefly moved his family there when he was born. Bruce Grobbelaar and Craig Johnston were in the Liverpool squad of the 1986 FA Cup Final. These players held a special place in the hearts of South African soccer fans and, even though they were White, were seen as flying the South African soccer flag high internationally. These players were very familiar to Mahobe, since each time he had travelled to England he had attended as many soccer matches as he could.

* * *

The Sundowns party touched down at Heathrow Airport on 9 May 1986. It was a Friday, and the FA Cup Final was going to be played the following day. There was much fanfare about that Cup Final. It was a Merseyside Derby – the name given to football matches between Everton (the Blues) and Liverpool (the Reds), both of which came from Liverpool, in the metropolitan county of Merseyside. The match was played seven days after Liverpool had secured the English Premier League title, with Everton finishing as runners-up. Liverpool were looking for a double title, while Everton were looking for revenge. Liverpool and Everton were widely regarded as the English league's leading club sides at the time.

On the day of the game, there was a carnival atmosphere in both Merseyside and London, with parties in many areas, and the blue and red team colours were everywhere. Posters and flags hung from windows, flags and streamers hung from the lampposts, and decorated tables were laid out along the streets and filled with buffet food. 'A brilliant day!' many called it. It was a brilliant day indeed, and Mahobe and the Sundowns party were there to be part of it, with many clad in their Sundowns T-shirts and waving Sundowns banners.

The game was played in front of a capacity crowd of 98 000 spectators and the atmosphere was electric. It was an exciting match, played at a great tempo. Everton took the lead in the 27th minute through a goal by Gary Lineker, after a 50-yard ball from Peter Reid over the top of the defenders, which Lineker chased, unleashing a shot at goal. Grobbelaar, the Liverpool goalkeeper, saved it, but it fell into Linekar's path and he directed it into the net. There was a thunderous cheer in the stadium from the Blues fans, as they chanted and waved their flags and banners high. The Liverpool fans looked stunned.

In the second half, Everton still had their tails up and were looking for that confidence-building second goal. First, Lineker fired wide, close to goal. Then Kevin Sheedy, after doing wonderful work tearing apart the defenders, fired a swerving ball close to the right goalpost. Sheedy fired again, with a free kick that sent Grobbelaar diving frantically to his left to deflect it. Everton definitely looked the more menacing of the two. But despite not having given Everton goalkeeper Bobby Mimms any nervous moments hitherto, it was Liverpool who drew first blood in the second half, with a wonderful goal by Ian Rush in the 56th minute. There was a thunderous roar from the Liverpool stands.

Mahobe and the rest of the Sundowns party were absorbing the atmosphere. It was what they had come to London to see, and the gods were giving it to them. Some cup finals can be a boring affair, but not this one. They were cheering at everything – the players, the electric atmosphere in the stadium, and even themselves, as they waved their Sundowns banners enthusiastically.

Game on. Score: 1–1. Tempo: very high. But the Blues still had their tails up and Grobbelaar had to make a great save when Graeme Sharp directed a header his way, which he did by deflecting it over the crossbar. It still looked like Everton were going to take it. But in the 62nd minute, the ball found Craig Johnston unmarked on the right, and he slotted home Liverpool's second goal.

In the 83rd minute, Everton were caught on a counter-attack, and Liverpool found themselves with acres of space, allowing Rush to score a third goal for Liverpool. This was after wonderful work first by Rush himself, then by Jan Molby, then Robbie Whelan and back to Rush to complete the loop and finish it off. The final score was 3–1 to Liverpool. They took home the trophy to make it a double title that year.

There were other memorable moments, too, during the match, such as the animated Bruce Grobbelaar's dramatic save of Sharp's header and the row he had with his defender, Jim Beglin. That was in the first half, and Everton were leading. The row began after Grobbelaar leapt for a swirling cross and dropped it. The ball was then played back into the box and as he tried to grab it again, Sharp kicked it out of his hands. Grobbelaar shouted at Beglin to leave the ball for him and rushed to the side of his box to get it. But without warning, Beglin trapped the ball as Grobbelaar skidded past helplessly. He was livid. He snatched up the ball and unloaded his fury into the Irishman's face from a distance of little more than an inch. He then furiously shoved him away, summoned him back, rolled the ball to his feet, demanded the ball back again, and scooped it up. There was a roar of laughter from the Everton fans.

It was mission accomplished for Mahobe, at least the first part of it. He had wanted his boys and his officials to see a great game of soccer, and that's exactly what they got. It was a final that would continue to stand out in the minds of many soccer followers for years to come.

To them, going to London was not only a soccer experience, but also a cultural experience. It was an experience of the world outside apartheid South Africa, especially of how the White people of England treated Black people. There was a degree of racism in England – quite a lot, in fact – but nothing compared to South Africa's apartheid. The English were mere snobs who regarded Blacks as lower class than haters who went out at night hunting for Blacks to kill. That evening, some of the guys went out to the nightclubs to celebrate, while others decided to stay at the hotel and have drinks at the bar. All conversations in London that night were about the Cup Final.

***

While in London, Sundowns, in contravention of the sports boycott on South Africa, trained with Crystal Palace and later played a match with them. They lost the match 2–1. The solitary goal for Sundowns was scored by Themba Ngwenya from a corner kick. Crystal Palace used one of their own coaches as the referee and replaced the goal posts with dustbins. In that way, the match could not be regarded as a FIFA-recognised game under its rules, and they could not be accused of breaking the football boycott.

The media loved Mahobe and Sundowns, and news soon travelled back home to South Africa that Sundowns had played a match with an English club, and in so doing had managed to defy the sports boycott against South Africa. Mark Gleeson, a sports reporter for the newspaper *The Star*, was part of the Sundowns party. Mahobe and his Mamelodi Sundowns were in the spotlight, dominating the media again.

The sports boycott of South Africa, although meant to punish the apartheid government, hurt the Blacks more than it did the Whites. Rugby and cricket always found ways to break the international sports boycott. A number of 'rebel' cricket teams such as those from Sri Lanka, West Indies, England, and Australia, and rebel rugby teams such as those from France, England, and Ireland, were enticed with substantial amounts of money to come and play against all-White 'national' teams in South Africa, in violation of the boycott. These teams would play unofficial internationals against Springbok teams, much to the disgust of the boycott movement.

The rugby Springboks also toured New Zealand in 1981, in what has been dubbed the 'Barbed Wire Tour', since it sparked mass protests and civil disobedience in New Zealand. Two games actually had to be cancelled. In one match, protesters tore down a chain fence, sprinkled nails all over the pitch and then staged a sit-in on the halfway line. Subsequent matches saw the arrival of barbed wire and police with batons. During the final test of the tour, a Cessna aircraft repeatedly dropped flour bombs, flares and leaflets onto the pitch. Subsequently, New Zealand cut sporting ties with South Africa until after the fall of apartheid.

Boxing somehow managed to partly escape the boycott. The South African Boxing Board of Control (SABBC) was expelled from the World Boxing Council (WBC) in 1975. However, the SABBC was affiliated with the WBC's popular rival, the World Boxing Association (WBA), which had not imposed bans on South African boxers. This resulted in the staging of international fights, such as that between Peter 'Terror' Mathebula and Tae Shik Kim in Los Angeles in 1980, which saw Mathebula being crowned the WBA flyweight world champion. Another memorable fight was that between American boxer John Tate and South African Gerrie Coetzee at Sun City in 1984, which Coetzee won by a knockout in the eighth round.

South African soccer could not do the same because of its stricter governing body, FIFA. No nation or recognised club dared to defy FIFA, for fear of being expelled. That was why Crystal Palace and Sundowns went to such lengths to make sure that their game could not be regarded as a proper soccer match recognisable by FIFA according to its laws.

Regardless, it was a small victory for Mahobe and Mamelodi Sundowns. He did not do it to defy the boycott movement, but to take a swipe at the apartheid authorities. But most of all, he was a developer. He had big dreams for Sundowns and for soccer in South Africa.

* * *

It was while he was in London that Mahobe had his first scare regarding his money dealings back home in South Africa. The guys and their partners, without Mahobe, had gone sightseeing in London, and the bus had stopped at an attraction so they could take photos. Stix and Gladys were just stepping out of the bus and were having a bitter quarrel.

'Come on, now, I am sick of this obsession of yours! I've heard enough of it. When are you going to stop it?' Stix shouted at Gladys.

'When are you going to stop feeling so sorry for yourself? It's that small mind of yours again playing tricks on you.'

'Stop calling me that!'

'Oh yes, but it's true.'

He grabbed her and started shoving her around. There were police passing by and they stopped to see what was happening. Stix was arrested.

Later that day Mahobe was confronted by police at the hotel. They found him sitting at the restaurant with Six.

'Are you Mr Mahobe?' they asked.

'Yes, I am, officers. Have I done something wrong?'

'We are going to ask you to come with us to the police station, sir.'

'Can I get something upstairs from my room quickly?'

'Yes, you can. You will find us waiting for you down here.'

He went upstairs to his room with Six. 'I am going to ask you to come with me in case it's something serious,' he said to him.

'I wonder what it could be,' said Six.

'Who knows? I just hope it is not what I am thinking.'

'And what's that?'

'Don't worry about it. If something happens, tell Jabu that he should handle everything from here.'

'I hope it is nothing serious.'

'Let's hope so.'

Indeed, it was nothing that concerned him. They told him that they had arrested Stix on a harassment charge and that he had asked them to get in touch with him as his employee. He was relieved – very relieved. He pleaded with them and also asked Gladys to withdraw the harassment charge, which she did, and Stix was released on a warning.

There were a few other incidents involving the couples in London that saw Mahobe having to spend extra money to maintain peace and stability. He even had to buy tickets for an early return for at least one wife or girlfriend.

Snowy had her fair share of troubles in London, too. The trip to London was not her first, so while the boys enjoyed sightseeing or doing whatever they wanted to do, Snowy and Gladys went shopping. Snowy had her own money and could afford expensive gifts for herself – especially beautiful shoes. Gladys also wanted to buy expensive things for herself in London, but she did not have the money. She tried to borrow money from Snowy – something she had done often enough before this trip. Snowy had always obliged, and Gladys had usually failed to pay her back. It was almost as if she had some kind of hold on Snowy – as if she knew something about her that other people did not know. Like it was some kind of blackmail. Snowy could not stomach it any more, and decided to put a stop to it.

'*Mngani wami*, this is getting too much,' she said to her. 'I have been lending you money for God knows how long now, and you have not paid me back a penny.'

'Please, *mngani*, just this one last time. I promise you I will pay you back.'

'And how exactly do you propose to do that?'

'I'll make a plan.'

'A plan doesn't do it for me. Where will you get the money?'

'From my boyfriend, of course.'

'Then I suggest you go and ask him for money now, because I'm not giving you a penny. You should have thought of that first, before begging from me.'

'So you think you're better because your boyfriend has money?' countered Gladys. 'Shame on you.'

'I am not spending Zola's money. I have my own money.'

'And where do you get it from? I know how much you earn and it's peanuts. You can't afford all this on your salary.'

'Why so nosy? It is none of your business where I get my money from. Besides, you know that I'm related to royalty in Lesotho.'

'So you think you have the right to treat me like trash?'

'You know what, *mngani*? I think you should stop making a fool of yourself, because it won't make me give you a penny.'

They stood there glaring at each other. Then Snowy waltzed out of the shop and took a taxi back to the hotel. That was the end of their calling each other *mngani*. The problem was that Snowy couldn't just wave goodbye to her former friend and never see her again – they shared the same office back home, and would have to continue working together. And Gladys would sit there wondering where Snowy got all her money from if it wasn't from Mahobe.

* * *

The Sundowns party arrived back in South Africa to a warm reception from fans and journalists. It was almost like welcoming a national team back home.

'We have had the most wonderful time in London. Everything went according to plan,' the proud Mahobe told the journalists.

'Is it true that you also had a practice match against Crystal Palace?' asked one journalist.

'It was not exactly a match, but just a practice session. We don't want to be on the wrong side of FIFA. But I must say that the boys enjoyed it immensely.'

As a publicity and branding exercise, the visit had been a triumph. No Black team had gone overseas to play a game, be it a practice game or a full international game, since the tour of England by the Orange Free State Bantu FC – dubbed the 'Kaffir

Football Team' by their overseas hosts – in 1898/99. They played 50 games against England, Scotland, Ireland, Wales and France.

And as a team-building exercise, it also had its benefits. Mike Ntombela, in his book *After the Fans Have Stopped Cheering*, said they came back stronger and more focused, leading to better performances in the league competition in subsequent seasons.

But people were beginning to ask questions. It was obvious that Mahobe had other sources of income outside his businesses. The players started to get uneasy. According to Ntombela, persistent questions from fans about Mahobe's magical rise to fame and fortune were unsettling, if not annoying.

The betrayal

– *Iphutha elikhulu*

After London, Mahobe started to work on another of his grandiose schemes. This time he planned to take the Mamelodi Sundowns players on a learning tour of the major soccer centres of Brazil. 'Ma-J, Ma-Six, Ma-Stix, the time has come to take the guys to Brazil,' he said to Jabu, Six and Stix during one of their briefing sessions. 'I want them to learn their game. They can dance; we can dance. They can dance the samba; we can dance the pata pata.'

Jabu, Six and Stix also did not know how Mahobe was making his millions. It was not their place to ask. Their motto was, 'If you don't know, then there is nothing to tell'. That way they could all stay protected. But he always insisted his money was coming from his businesses.

He let his travel agency, Via Africa, start work on the travel plans. But all the brouhaha about the trip forewarned the Brazilian consulate in Botswana, and they were refused visas. Brazil had ended diplomatic relations with South Africa in 1985, and had even imposed sanctions against the country in protest against apartheid.

In the same year, they opened a consulate in Botswana. Mahobe and his travel party were disappointed. More than England, Brazil was the place he wanted to take his players.

Many suspected interference by the apartheid South African government in the refusal of the visas, but it is generally accepted that they were refused because of the sports boycott against South Africa. The stunt that Mahobe had pulled in London was not going to happen in Brazil. After all, the president of FIFA at the time, João Havelange, was a Brazilian.

The sports boycott had earlier turned into big news around the world when Zola Budd, a White athlete from Bloemfontein, broke the women's 5 000 m world record. The performance was not recognised because it took place in apartheid South Africa. She later obtained a hurriedly arranged British citizenship and made headlines during the 1984 Los Angeles Summer Olympics when she tragically collided with American medal hopeful Mary Decker. The two had been on everybody's lips during the build-up to the Olympics, with some predicting that Budd would win it and others supporting Decker. Budd ran barefoot, while Decker wore spikes. Budd, while attempting to take the lead, cut in front of Decker and collided with her. Their hopes melted into tears. Later, Budd came back to South Africa and had an excellent season in 1991, when she was the second-fastest woman in the world over 3 000 m.

News of his plans to take the team to Brazil so soon after London made the alarm bells ring louder around Mahobe. More people started questioning whether his businesses could sustain his lifestyle, while to others he was an apartheid-era hero who was doing good things for the South African people, especially soccer fans. The latter did not care where the money came from, as long as he continued to do 'the Lord's things' with it. Nobody knew where many of the Black apartheid-era tycoons got the money to start their businesses from, or whether their wealth came solely from their businesses; nobody cared.

Despite the money alarms going off, the people at Standard Bank, where Mahobe kept his cash, slept peacefully. They knew him only as one of their valued clients and had not made the connection between him and their faithful employee, Tebello Snowy Moshoeshoe.

* * *

Gladys knew that Mahobe and Snowy must have been doing something illegal. Why was Snowy still working at the bank when her salary could not pay for her lifestyle? Why was she still working there when her boyfriend, who was willing to do anything for her, had so much money? He was even giving away some of it to his players, officials, and ordinary people. Overseas trips, expensive cars, houses, gifts, financial bailouts. She wanted in, but Snowy would not admit her. In fact, since their fallout in London, they had been engaged in a cold war.

In the office they shared, Gladys did paperwork and Snowy worked on the computers.

'*Mngani*, can you show me how to work the computers?' asked Gladys one day. This took Snowy by surprise, especially since their relationship had gone sour. She was saying it on purpose. What was she playing at?

'Haibo! You know I can't do that,' she said.

'Just curious. Bet you could manipulate the computers if you wanted to.'

'Why would I do that? And please don't play buddy-buddy with me. We both know that we aren't buddies any more.'

But she knew that Gladys was onto her.

Thoughts of vindication started to build up inside Gladys. Queen Snowy had to pay. She wanted a way of anonymously whispering to someone in management that Snowy was Mahobe's girlfriend, so that they could make the connection between his extravagant lifestyle and the bank. Her chance came when Mahobe and Snowy appeared on the cover of the *Mamelodi Sundowns Magazine*.

The magazine feature provided her with the opportunity she had been looking for. It had everything about Mahobe and Snowy's extravagant lifestyle, including the trip to London and the foiled plan to tour Brazil. It was all there. All she had to do was to draw the attention of the Standard Bank managers to it. But she had a problem: not many White people read 'Black' magazines. But maybe the picture of Snowy on the cover would attract their attention.

She took the magazine to work, but she did not know how to draw the managers' attention to it. She kept it in her desk drawer for days, thinking about how to do it. Should she just leave it on top of the desk? But the managers hardly ever gave her a glimpse. They came to the office now and then, but it was to Snowy's workstation that they went. They usually didn't pay much attention to her. She also had another problem: even if she put it on the desk, how was she going to do it without Snowy noticing?

Then one day she left work late. Before she left she had been looking at the magazine, contemplating what to do, and she left it on top of her desk by mistake. The following day Snowy arrived earlier and discovered the magazine. She got a fright. What was Gladys up to? She was still standing next to the desk and staring at it, wide-eyed, when Gladys walked into the office. With hands trembling, Gladys quickly grabbed it and walked out of the office. She did not say hello. Finding the nearest wastepaper bin, she tore up the magazine and disposed of it. They never talked about it, but the tension was there, and it was unbearable. Snowy knew that Gladys was onto her. Should she confront her? She did not.

But Gladys went looking for another copy of the magazine. Her boyfriend, Stix, had many copies of the magazine at his place. One day she was summoned to the office of one of the managers and immediately she saw the opportunity she had been looking for. With Snowy looking on, she pulled open the drawer of her desk, took out the magazine, and carried it with her to the manager's office. Snowy was horrified. Gladys was finally doing it.

Gladys came back without the magazine. Snowy did not ask anything. She knew it was done; her world was beginning to turn upside down. Her head was spinning. She felt a cold trickle of sweat run down her left armpit and disappear somewhere. She needed something to drink. She left her desk and went to the kitchen to get some water. The seed had been planted. All that mattered now was whether it had been planted in fertile ground.

Gladys was in luck. The manager noticed Snowy on the cover and started reading the feature on her and Mahobe. Then the bells finally started to ring at Standard Bank. They started getting curious, asking more and more questions about Mahobe and Snowy's lives.

'How can she live such a glamorous life on just R700 a month?' asked one of the bank managers.

'Just look at her clothes,' said another. 'How does she pay for all that? Or is it her boyfriend who is doing the paying? Mind you, they have just come back from London, where the boyfriend took the whole team and officials and their spouses on an all-expenses-paid trip. If they love each other so much, what is she still working for as an office clerk?'

'Maybe she just needs the job to keep busy.'

'I doubt it. Something isn't right.'

'Have you ever asked yourself where her boyfriend gets all the money from?'

'I hear he is a businessman. But, goodness, to spend money like that!'

There were so many questions.

The end of the game
– *Sisenkingeni*

It was Mahobe's extravagant tastes that ultimately enabled Standard Bank to join the dots. He had driven the Mercedes 500 SL convertible and tired of it, then bought other luxury cars, which had also soon bored him. Now he wanted something different. He wanted to be elevated to the echelons of the rich and famous. So he decided he was going to treat himself to a new-generation Mercedes-Benz 500 SEL. Movie stars, presidents, and other celebrities loved to be driven in this model. He decided it was an appropriate image for him, now that he was a famous soccer boss.

Dealers in South Africa did not have stock of the 500 SEL with the specifications that he wanted, so in May 1987 he travelled to Germany and approached Mercedes-Benz there to order the car. But because of logistical complications, including warranty issues and the weak rand exchange rate, he was advised to buy the car through an agent in South Africa. Then Mercedes in Germany contacted its agent in South Africa to facilitate the deal. In turn, the local agent notified Mahobe's bank – Standard Bank – of the impending transaction.

But Mahobe did not have that kind of money in the account that he was using to purchase the car, and Standard Bank knew that something was wrong. By then the managers were watching Snowy like a hawk, and as soon as they got notification of the impending transaction, they struck.

She arrived at work one Friday only to be told to go back home. She knew something was wrong. Normally a credit enquiry of this nature would go through her and, according to the arrangement between her and Mahobe, she was meant to be there to facilitate it. She tried to resist, telling them that she did not need leave, but they insisted. They weren't just being nice and giving her some time off; something was wrong.

Mahobe was back from Germany and was in his office at Power Promotions. She called and told him what had happened. He was silent for a long time. 'Did they say why you must be on leave?'

'No. They say they will tell me when to go back. I'm scared.'

Mahobe was silent again, and her heart fell. 'This might be a problem,' he said.

'Just cancel the purchase,' said Snowy. 'You don't need a new car, anyway.'

'It's too late. Everything has been signed and the cheque must be at the bank already. We can't stop this.'

Now it was Snowy who was silent, as she pictured the train smash that was about to happen. Her world exploding. Gladys grinning triumphantly.

'Don't worry,' said Mahobe. 'I'll think of something. Just go home. Be cool. Leave it up to me.'

Mahobe got in his car and drove to Durban, where Sundowns were playing Bush Bucks that weekend. He needed the distraction and some time to think.

After the game, he called Snowy and told her he was going to stay in Durban for a while. He needed more time to come up with a plan. 'No need to worry,' he said. 'If anything happens, I have the best lawyers in the business. Trust me.'

Snowy didn't have to wait long for confirmation that the game was up. On a Monday morning near the end of May 1987 she was startled by a loud banging at the door and the dreaded words 'This is the police; open the door!' There was nowhere to run or hide. She had already resigned herself to getting arrested. She had expected it, but not so soon. A warrant of arrest for Mahobe was also issued on that day, but he was nowhere to be found. The last time anyone had seen him was at the Sundowns game against Bush Bucks in Durban on Saturday, 23 May.

Mahobe had been in Durban trying to decide what to do next. He needed a plan. But the only plan he came up with was that he needed to hide. So after the match he got in his car and drove straight to the stables in Khayalami, where he kept his racehorse. He had a room there with a fully stocked bar and a bathroom, where he used to entertain his friends when he wanted to show off his racehorse. He always found a way of making himself comfortable.

He was with Stix, who was the only one who knew where he was hiding. Stix went in and out of the stables to buy provisions, clothes and other essentials. Meanwhile, the workers and trainers went about their business without a thought for Mahobe. They were used to him pitching up at the stables without warning. Nobody knew that he was a wanted man.

'Ma-Stix, whatever you do, don't tell Snowy where I am,' he said to Stix. 'I am not sure she can handle the pressure, and she might lead them to me.'

'What about Six and Jabu; do you think I should tell them where you are?'

'I'm not so sure you should tell them. You are the only person who knows where I am, and I think we should keep it that way.'

Stix nodded his agreement. The police were talking to everyone in Mahobe's circle, so the fewer who knew his whereabouts the better.

'I'm missing Snowy; damn it!' said Mahobe. 'I want you to visit her where they are holding her and tell her that I am safe. Tell her that I love her. Be careful about it. Tell her that I used an untraceable telephone number to call you, or something, and that you also do not know where I am.'

'Yes, OK,' said Stix. 'But you know you can't stay here forever. Unless you work in the stables, you know, with blue overalls and everything.'

Mahobe laughed. 'That's a good plan, but, you know, it's not my style.'

Stix laughed at the thought of Mr Sundowns cleaning out the stables. It just wasn't gonna happen. 'Then, my brother, you must leave the country. Go to Mexico or somewhere. Like in the movies.'

Mahobe sat silently for a moment with a faraway expression. 'That's what I was thinking,' he said. 'We have our own Mexico right here. It's called Botswana. I will run off to Botswana.'

'Are you joking now?'

'For real. You must go to Pat. He can arrange it. But I must leave tomorrow.'

Pat was Mahobe's friend and was from Botswana. The last time they were together was before Pat had gone off in one of his cars with shoeboxes full of cash in the boot. It was not uncommon for Mahobe's cars to have lots of cash in the boot. Mahobe, Jabu, Pat, Six, and a few other friends had been having lunch in town at Wimpy – the one at the top of the Carlton Centre office building. It was one of the few places where Blacks could sit together with Whites, because the building had 'international' status. Mahobe had just bought another BMW 3 Series. Pat had asked whether he could test-drive the car and Mahobe had agreed. But Pat had never come back – he didn't give anyone a call; nothing. He must have driven it to Botswana and registered it there. It was very easy to register illegal cars in neighbouring countries back then. He would have known that Mahobe would not report it as stolen, so it would not be a wanted car. He would not have had to tamper with the car in any way; all he needed to do was to get it registered in his name. Mahobe could have made a big deal about it, but instead he had decided not to make a big deal of it because Pat ran his liquor outlets in Botswana.

'He is where he is because of me,' Mahobe now said, referring to Pat. 'And he's been helping himself to my profits in Botswana. So he owes me. Make sure he understands that.'

* * *

Stix was at the Kopfontein border post between Botswana and South Africa five minutes before it opened. It was only about 22 km to Gaborone from Kopfontein, so he would be at Pat's house in fifteen minutes or so.

As soon as he crossed the border into Botswana, he made a call from a telephone booth and told Pat he'd be at his house in fifteen minutes. He didn't give any other details.

When Stix arrived, Pat was having breakfast.

'Join me,' he said. 'I'm sure you haven't had anything to eat.'

'You're right. In fact, I didn't even have dinner last night. I was with Zola until late and had to drive straight here.'

'Well, if he's sent you here for money, the answer is no. I'm the one who is running the businesses now and their successes are due to my efforts. If it wasn't for me, they would be dead by now. I can't be his slave forever.'

'Take it easy, broer. It's not about money. He needs to come here on an urgent business trip.'

'So let him come. I'll supply the brandy.'

'Ja, see, bra Pat, it's not that simple. This business trip – let's just say the police can't know about it. So he can't use his passport.'

Pat sat back and laughed. 'So what you're saying is that Mr Big has finally gone and blown it and he's on the run.'

Stix shrugged. 'Something like that. Now can you help?'

Pat finished the last of his breakfast, taking his time. 'Do you want some coffee?' he said. 'You look tired.'

'No. Just tell me if you can help.'

'I don't know,' said Pat. 'These illegal things, they're bad for business. And the South African Police. I mean, why are you playing games with them now?'

Stix was silent, knowing that the man was enjoying his moment of power.

'OK, look, I'll see what I can do,' said Pat after carrying his empty plate to the kitchen. 'But it can't be for tonight. It will have to be first thing the day after tomorrow. I will have to organise him a used Botswana passport. My men will meet you on the South African side of the border and hand over the passport. Now you must go back home and send me passport-size photos of him by courier.'

Stix breathed a sigh of relief. 'Thanks, bra Pat, this means everything to me.'

With puffy eyes and head spinning, Stix drove like a madman back to South Africa. When he arrived at Mahobe's hideout, they started to make arrangements.

'They don't usually have roadblocks after midnight,' said Stix. 'We'll have to leave around that time.'

'In the meantime, I want you to go and organise me some money,' said Mahobe. 'Go and find Jabu and speak to him. He'll know what to do.'

Stix went to Jabu and he managed to put together about R30 000 in a hurry. He also tried hard to get Stix to tell him where Mahobe was hiding, but he wouldn't.

A few minutes after midnight they left Mahobe's hideout and headed for Botswana. The journey to the border took what seemed like forever to Mahobe. There was a full moon and not a cloud in the sky.

'What do you think, Ma-Stix; why do you think the moon is shining so bright?'

'Because it is full moon; why else?'

'I think the heavens are trying to expose me. There is not a cloud in the sky. Or is it a sign of freedom – a signal that I am going to be free where I am going?'

As he finished saying this, they heard a police siren wailing in the distance and getting louder and louder. 'What is that now?

Damn it!' swore Mahobe. The police van was getting closer and closer to them. 'Maybe you should stop the car.'

'No need to. They'll let us know if they want us to pull over. If we stop, we'll look suspicious.'

The van whizzed past them, travelling at high speed. His heart was almost in his throat. He could only breathe easily again when they came in sight of the border.

As usual, there were the early birds already waiting on the South African side for the Kopfontein border to open. Stix called Pat from a phone booth.

'My men are waiting for you,' said Pat. 'Go to your car and stand next to it and light up a cigarette. That's the sign; they'll come to you and ask for a cigarette. Leave the car windows open.'

Stix went to the car and did as instructed. Then two men approached the car and one of them asked him for a cigarette. As he handed it to him, the other one dropped the passport into the car. Mahobe recognised them. These were the same connections they used to use in the days when he was still working underground for the PAC.

Snowy's trial

– *Kuqulwa izesekeli*

Snowy was trembling. It had never occurred to her that they would one day get caught. It did not take long for the trial to begin. The day after her arrest, Snowy was taken to the Rand Supreme Court in Johannesburg, where she and Mahobe were accused of defrauding Standard Bank of more than R10 million, a vast sum of money in those days (equivalent to more than R122 million in 2022). According to Standard Bank, the actual figure was believed to be as much as R10,3 million.

The court heard how Snowy had been regarded by her colleagues as a willing, highly cooperative, highly skilled, and pleasant employee, and how the bank had relied on her skills so much that she had hardly ever taken leave. It was only later that the bank had discovered that she and her lover, Mahobe, had been living a lavish lifestyle at their expense. According to the evidence, most of the money had been diverted into Mahobe's accounts at various branches of Standard Bank. The method she had used involved injecting fictitious credits into the system, offsetting them via inter-branch transaction accounts, and then forging signatures on replies to enquiries. This revealed her extraordinary grasp of the intricacies of the accounting system – something that they had not expected of her. Of course, Mahobe had taught her all this. She had done it until a few days before her arrest.

She did not offer much resistance during her trial; all the evidence was there. The soccer world at large was stunned, though some of those close to her and Mahobe were probably not too surprised. It was also soon public knowledge that a warrant of arrest had been issued for Mahobe and that he was nowhere to be found. Instead of being outraged at the fact that Mahobe had built Sundowns on wealth acquired illegally, many Blacks were angry that he had been found out. It was hard to imagine Sundowns without him, and the fans missed him. At a Sundowns game played at HM Pitje Stadium on 31 May 1987, the fans chanted 'Viva Zola, Viva!' as the team beat Rangers 2–1, with Bennet Masinga scoring a brace.

In August 1987, Snowy, then 28 years old, was convicted on 129 counts of fraud and sentenced to ten years in prison, of which she served only four.

'I am not a thief,' she told the court. 'I was only taking instructions from my boyfriend. I made the transfers whenever he instructed me to.'

But the court was buying none of it – she was not a naive teenager taking instructions from her gangster sugar daddy.

The estates of Mahobe and Snowy were finally sequestrated in the Rand Supreme Court. But they could not touch the house in Rockville because it was not registered in Mahobe's name. They also could not touch his businesses in Durban and Pietersburg because they were also not registered in his name.

* * *

Snowy was to serve her time at the Female Centre of the Johannesburg Prison, commonly known as Sun City Prison. It was known as one of the most dangerous female prisons in South Africa. Some inmates were known to possess dangerous weapons, putting other inmates' lives at risk.

Johannesburg Prison came to be called Sun City after the well-known casino resort in Bophuthatswana (now part of North West). Compared with other prisons, it was said to be modern, with beds, linen, hot water, and showers. The food was also said to be better than that of most prisons.

But the food and the linen and the hot water were just things, not people. Sun City Prison was no bed of roses. The warders were rude and frequently abused prisoners, both verbally and physically. Long-term inmates did the same to new arrivals, sometimes making them handle their own excrement. Non-consensual sex acts were also rife, and hardened criminals serving long sentences would force new, young inmates into being their 'wives'. They would protect them from harm, provide them with little luxuries such as food, blankets, or cash, and expect faithfulness in return. If the wife was caught cheating, she would be punished and disciplined. It was even worse with the male prisoners at Sun City. The prison officials knew about these acts, but they did nothing about them.

Snowy had been to the real Sun City Resort many times, and this was no Sun City Resort. This was going to be her home for the next few years. Welcome to Sun City.

She was scared of the prison and the things she saw happening to other inmates. But she was lucky. Many warders and inmates knew who she was; her case was the most talked-about issue in the country. They hero-worshipped her. The White warders worshipped her too.

She did get some abuse, such as someone trying to make her their wife or trying to pick a fight with her. But once they got to know who she was, they would stop. Soon, everybody knew who she was and all the abuse stopped. Instead, she became a friend who comforted others and was someone they could confide in. It kept her mind occupied. It gave her purpose in life. She knew that things would never be the same again.

Standard Bank takes over Sundowns

– Iphuciwe

With Mahobe's fraud exposed, Standard Bank found itself the surprised caretakers of a soccer club. Don Macey, an experienced soccer administrator, referee and special projects manager who acted on behalf of the bank, made sure that the players were taken care of and was working on preventing the club from being dissolved. The interim committee appointed to run Sundowns was keeping him informed of the negotiations. At the time, Mike Ntombela was the team captain, and his job was to motivate the players.

Standard Bank faced a dilemma. It could disband the club and sell off the players to recover some of the money that Mahobe had stolen from them, or they could sell the entire club. They decided on the latter. Colin Fisher, the appointed trustee from Coopers & Lybrand, was giving serious consideration to a meagre offer of R10 000 made by Drs Itsweng and Sebotsane, who also wanted

Standard Bank to become sponsors of the club. The offer was not acceptable to the bank, however, and they were also not willing to take on the sponsorship commitment. It was Don Macey who advised the bank that the club was worth considerably more than the sum being offered. It was then decided that they would keep the team running while awaiting acceptable offers.

The bank did not want to dispose of Sundowns in a careless manner. They could have sold its players and recovered some of the stolen money, but they were conscious of how huge the club was and what it meant to Black communities, especially that of Mamelodi. Getting rid of it irresponsibly would have been bound to taint the bank's image in these communities. This left only the option of keeping the club running until a solution could be found. Don Macey managed the club effectively throughout the 1988 season. Screamer Tshabalala – the coach – became the face of Sundowns, and Trott Moloto became the assistant coach.

Tshabalala left the club that year after a fall out with the players. He had cost them a place in the JPS Knockout competition by fielding a player who was on four yellow cards in a game they won. As a result, the game had to be replayed, and they lost the replay. This was not the only incident that had made the players unhappy with Tshabalala. There were others.

Another problem was that Tshabalala was both manager and coach of the club. The players had mixed feelings about him. They feared him, yet they played for him. This was a peculiar situation in soccer. There had been instances where players had the roles of both player and coach, but this – manager and coach – was something unheard of. The trust deficit between him and the players grew and became so large that he eventually had to tender his resignation. After his departure, Mario Tuani, a former Moroka

Swallows coach, became the new head coach. Angelo Tsichlas, a former goalkeeper for Greek side Atromitos and assistant coach to Tuani at Moroka Swallows, became the goalkeeper mentor.

Despite being rocked by the disclosure of Mahobe's fraud and the abrupt change of ownership, Sundowns kept their eyes focused on the prize – the 1987 NSL league championship. The Mahobe effect was still alive in them. They led for most of the way, and only Chiefs looked capable of mounting a strong enough challenge to edge them out. In their first 21 games, Sundowns lost only twice: 0–1 to AmaZulu and a shocking 0–5 to Hellenic.

But after mid-August the Mahobe effect began to wear off, and of their remaining thirteen games they won only three, losing five and drawing five. The title was decided in the last match of the season, and it was Jomo Cosmos who finally emerged the victors with 46 points, edging out Kaizer Chiefs, who had been leading until that last match, by a point. Sundowns ended third, with 43 points. Would they have won the league if Mahobe and Snowy had not been caught out?

Mahobe's arrest
– Iqhawe elingumkhwabanisi

While all this was going on, there was still one big question on everyone's mind – where was the mastermind, the legend, the man with the plan who had made all the fireworks happen? Sundowns players, soccer lovers, friends, investors, journalists, the shocked public and the police were all pondering the matter deeply. Since Mahobe had left that Bush Bucks game in Durban, the only person in South Africa who had seen him was Stix, and he was keeping dead quiet about that fact.

Mahobe was still in Botswana, where he was receiving financial support from his close friends and associates, channelled through Six. There were still those businesses that were not registered under his name, which Standard Bank had missed in trying to recover its money, and Six was collecting money from some of them and passing it on to Mahobe.

In June 1987, the South African Police and Standard Bank offered a reward of R10 000 for information leading to Mahobe's arrest. In August, the reward was increased to R50 000 (equivalent to more than half a million rand in 2022). Now it was becoming tempting. Pat sat looking at Mahobe and started seeing a nice, plump retirement fund just waiting to be pocketed. Besides, he had no more use for Mahobe now, and was making himself an accomplice by harbouring him. He thought he'd give himself a few days to think about it, but then he snapped out of it – that money was going to be a temptation to even the best of Mahobe's friends. He had to act quickly.

Pat had connections in high places, people who shared his eye for a ripe opportunity. Some of those connections happened to be high-ranking police officers. So he approached one of them and told them what he knew. Shortly afterwards, a message was sent to the South African Police. The South African authorities then made a formal request to the Botswana government to have Mahobe arrested and handed over.

* * *

Since he had arrived in Botswana, Mahobe had developed a habit of jogging in the mornings to keep fit and clear his head. Pat would sometimes drive over to his place and join him. On 27 January 1988, Pat arrived early to join him for a jog. Mahobe was glad to see him and off they went. It was a beautiful, sunny Wednesday morning and the harsh Botswana summer heat had not made its presence felt yet. They jogged and chatted for about an hour before getting back to Mahobe's place and sitting down to some breakfast. They had hardly begun when there was a knock on the door.

'Are you expecting someone?' asked Pat.

'No. Let me see who it is,' said Mahobe as he made his way to the door. He opened the door and found an armed policeman standing there.

'Are you Mr Mahobe?' asked the policeman.

Mahobe started to feel weak at the knees. His head started spinning. 'Yes, I am, why?'

'Sir, we would like you to come to the station with us.'

Mahobe looked past the policeman and saw three police vehicles, with five police officers armed with shotguns and rifles. The house was surrounded.

'What's happening, officers?' asked Pat, disingenuously.

'We are taking Mr Mahobe with us to the station. You can follow us there if you want. There is something we need to talk to him about.'

Mahobe went with the police, still wearing his tracksuit and running shoes. Pat followed him to the police station, still pretending not to know anything about the arrest.

Two days later, the Botswana police handed Mahobe over to the South African authorities. He had been a fugitive for over eight months. Apart from pocketing the R50 000, Pat also 'inherited' Mahobe's businesses.

The trial

– Viva Zola

Mahobe's trial began at the Johannesburg Regional Court on 8 July 1988, where he was charged with five counts of theft, involving R6 037 870 of the R10 315 000 allegedly taken from the bank. He was represented by the law firm Maluleke, Seriti and Moseneke. There was no denying the crime, since Snowy had already spilt the beans. All his defence could do was fight for a lighter sentence. The charges related to 93 fraudulent transactions that took place between 3 February 1983 and 9 May 1987.

The charges highlighted the significance of 1983 in Mahobe's life. It was in 1983 that he convinced Snowy to leave her job as a nurse at Leratong Hospital and get a job at Standard Bank. Shortly after that, his businesses started to grow at those too-good-to-be-true rates, and he began splashing out cash like a king and mingling with A-list celebrities. That was also the year he said, when being asked about his almost magical rise to fame and fortune, 'I have made a lot of ground in business because I don't hesitate when I want something'.

Mahobe was held at Sun City Prison during his trial – a stone's throw away from the Kaizer Chiefs training grounds in Naturena. He hated it. Motaung was still out there, enjoying the glamourous life of soccer, while he was cooped up in this hole with no hope of escaping. The male section of Sun City Prison was notorious for its violence, including and the bullying of inmates – especially new ones – and other despicable acts. But Mahobe experienced none of it. He was the 'Big Boss'. He was regarded as a Robin Hood, even by the prisoners. They adored him, and everybody wanted to be his friend.

Besides, gangsters were feared, and they regarded Mahobe as a gangster. Gangsters had connections all over, including in prison. Some of the warders were also on their payroll. Things happened to those who crossed their paths, and there were even inmates who lost their lives because they got on the wrong side of a gang member. Nobody touched Mahobe, neither an inmate nor a warder.

The court case attracted a lot of media attention in South Africa and neighbouring states, as well as in England and Australia. Everybody in South Africa was talking about it. Mahobe pleaded not guilty, claiming he did not know the funds in his accounts had been fraudulently deposited by Snowy. He told the court it was his belief that Snowy had received the money from farms and properties sold in Lesotho by her relatives, headed by King Moshoeshoe II, and that the money was a loan to him. This line of argument was extremely flimsy, considering that Snowy had already confessed to depositing money fraudulently into his accounts whenever he asked her to.

He also told the court that he had remained in Botswana for eight months after charges were laid against him in South Africa because he was 'sick from the shock' of his being a wanted man. But the judge wasn't buying it.

The court was full each time Mahobe appeared. The story was also big in the print media. There would not be a newspaper left to buy in the townships after ten in the morning. Conversations everywhere were about Mahobe – in the buses, trains, minibus taxis, shebeens, newspapers and magazines, on radio, and wherever two or more people were gathered. People loved him for his sense of fearlessness in those times when instilling fear in Black people was the biggest weapon at the disposal of the apartheid regime. He was also highly intelligent. He had patiently planned and learnt over the years until he got it right. How did it occur to him to do what he had done? No such crime had ever been committed in the world. The fact that he was a Black in apartheid South Africa made it even more fascinating. Some who had not seen him in person before wanted to be there to see him. They wanted to see this Black Robin Hood who was able to take so much money from the rich Whites, not to keep it all for himself but to enjoy it with the people.

This was another big bank robbery story to come out of South Africa, following that of André Stander and his gang. Between 1977 and 1980, they robbed nearly 30 banks by the simple method of walking in and demanding that the tellers hand over the cash. Sometimes they robbed three or four banks in a day, and are even said to have robbed the same bank twice in one day. According to Allan Heyl, one of the gang members, sometimes the security guards at the banks would even open the doors for them, not knowing that they had just robbed the bank. Stander, a former policeman, claimed that his lawlessness was a result of disillusionment with the police after the 1976 Soweto riots.

Mahobe, ever true to his character, was not going to disappoint his admirers when he appeared in court. He had to look good in front of them. He also knew that his picture would be on TV and in the newspapers, and he wanted to look good for the cameras. Each time before he appeared in court they would bring him smart clothes to wear – at least two outfits to choose from. It was a glamour show; a high-society court case. It kept the people glued to their TVs, radios and newspapers.

Magistrate Booysens had a hard time controlling the noise each time Mahobe walked into the courtroom or said something funny – like when he said he had thought the money in his accounts was coming from the sale of farms and land by the royal family in Lesotho.

'Viva Zola! Viva Zola!' they chanted.

Magistrate Booysens would threaten them and order 'Silence in the court!' but they would continue chanting until they decided it was time to get on with the show. The court precinct was also abuzz with Mahobe's supporters.

Black people, especially soccer fans, did not want him to be found guilty. His crime was almost politicised, considering the fact that, at the time, stealing from the rich Whites was not considered much of a crime by most Black people, and also that Mahobe had spent a lot of the money on creating a team that the people loved. They needed many Mahobes – more Black Robin Hoods.

* * *

While Mahobe's trial was going on, his close friends were scratching their heads, trying to figure out a way to get him off the hook. Even though the evidence against him was overwhelming, they never lost hope. They needed a miracle worker – someone who could make the case turn in Mahobe's favour. They heard about a popular sangoma by the name of Mangconde in Umtata in Transkei (now part of the Eastern Cape) and decided to visit her.

Mangconde's clients included all sorts of people – the rich, the famous, and the very ordinary. She even had White clients. That's how powerful and well known she was. When the delegation from Johannesburg arrived, she said, 'I know why you came here. You have a difficult court case that you want me to help you with'. She then performed some rituals and told them to go back to Johannesburg. 'Things will work out in your favour.'

But time passed and nothing was changing for Mahobe. On the contrary, things seemed to be getting worse for him. His friends then decided to go to his muthi man in Vereeniging – the one who also used to be the muthi man for Sundowns. His name was Khoza. Khoza was known among his clients to be a very powerful muthi man. He asked that Mahobe's friends bring him a tray of six eggs. This they did. Then he smeared the eggs with muthi and performed a ritual. He gave them back the eggs and told them that on the next day of Mahobe's court appearance they should place them along the path of the police truck taking him to court, and that if the truck drove over them and broke them, then Mahobe's case would be thrown out of court – broken, so to speak. It was a tricky affair – something that could even end in someone getting killed, should the police driving the truck spot someone placing an object in its way. What if it was a bomb? However, on the next court date, Mahobe's friends appointed someone to perform the task, and they managed to place the small tray of eggs in the path of the truck a short distance from the Sun City Prison entrance.

But none of Khoza's claims materialised. Time passed and things were getting worse for Mahobe. It seemed there was no saving him from a prison term.

The use of muthi in soccer was not uncommon. One goalkeeper (not from Sundowns) has jokingly related a story of how each time their muthi man was having a session with them, he would hide his gloves, because the muthi man used to smear them with a slippery ointment, claiming that it would make the ball stick on them. The use of muthi was also common in teams such as Orlando Pirates, whose players would jump over fires at a sangoma's house on Friday nights ahead of the Soweto Derby. The muthi man of Jomo Cosmos would spray a white substance on the floor leading to their dressing room at their home ground in Springs. This put the 'fear of the devil' into opposing teams. In fact, almost every first division team used muthi, whether it was the team as a whole or the individual players. But not all the players believed in it.

* * *

Once all the muthi and magic and creative storytelling were over, it was time for judgement. In his summing-up, presented to a packed courtroom, Magistrate Booysens told Mahobe that his claim that he thought the funds deposited into his various business bank accounts were loans from the Lesotho royal family was false beyond reasonable doubt. He also found it far-fetched that Mahobe had been 'sick from the shock' of being a wanted man. On 12 January 1989, the magistrate sentenced Mahobe to a total of 29 years in prison, after finding him guilty on all five counts of theft. Thirteen years of the sentence were to run concurrently, giving him an effective sixteen years' imprisonment. In the end, he served only five of the sixteen years.

There was no great sense of outrage among Black people when Mahobe and Snowy's scheme was exposed. People were more interested in the glamour aspect of the story and the sophisticated and daring nature of the crime, rather than in making great moral judgements. Also, to many, he was someone who was taking money from the racist White government to spend it on his oppressed people. To them he was the Robin Hood of apartheid-era South Africa, and they felt the sentence was too harsh.

According to White circles outside South Africa, Mahobe and Snowy were a reflection of the sophisticated, confident, emerging Black South African elite who knew that apartheid was being forced out of existence. Black people were refusing to accept White authority. As a result, when news of Mahobe and Snowy's crime broke, there was very little unease about its illegality in these White circles. Things like selling through the 'back door' or stealing from the Whites were long-established practices dating back to the times when Blacks moved to cities such as Johannesburg to seek better opportunities. The 'Black Robin Hoods' of Sophiatown had started it, and it continued to be common in Soweto. Mahobe and Snowy were just taking it to another level. There were huge arguments about whether this crime should be applauded or not. The feeling was that this was wrong but, on the other hand, it had been a *lekker klap* in the faces of the apartheid masters.

'Then we'll have to extend the definition of criminality,' said someone during a discussion about Mahobe. 'You know, like we have a lie and a white lie. Zola had the brains, the balls, and the opportunity to take just a little from the oppressors, and look how he distributed it among the Black people. He gave it to his players, his officials, his staff, his friends, and ordinary people in need. Is that an act of a criminal? No. He was not a criminal. He was an activist.'

As Mike Ntombela put it, 'Politically, after the Boers had taken our land, they had stolen what is more significant. I want you to tell this story. Not that I am saying stealing is right. You see, stealing during those times was not stealing.'

The Tsichlases and the Krok brothers
– Kuphethe abasha

There was panic in the Sundowns camp and among soccer fans during the trial, but the provisional trustee of Mahobe's estate – Standard Bank – assured the public that negotiations were underway to keep the club running. This was a great relief to soccer fans. An interim committee was appointed to run Sundowns and the team didn't stop playing. The members of the committee were attorney Willie Seriti, Dr Motsiri Itsweng, Dr Bonny Sebotsane, Ngamula Malewa (the team's PRO), and Screamer Tshabalala (the coach).

In April 1988 Don Macey of Standard Bank arranged a public meeting in Mamelodi, which was attended by about 2 000 Sundowns supporters. The purpose of the meeting was to explain the bank's policy to the supporters and assure them that, although they could not take on a sponsorship commitment, they would not dispose of the club irresponsibly and would give the local community a three-month option to put together a suitable offer. But they could not. There was considerable enthusiasm and goodwill from the supporters towards the bank. At one game against Kaizer Chiefs at Atteridgeville Stadium, the crowd was estimated at 45 000 – far in excess of the stadium's capacity.

The plan that Standard Bank was working on to keep Sundowns alive was taking shape in ongoing discussions between the Krok brothers and Angelo and Anastasia Tsichlas for the sale of the team. Word in the soccer circles had it that Irvin Khoza was also interested in buying Sundowns, but Kaizer Motaung, a former Orlando Pirates player and friend, advised him to rather concentrate on bringing the ailing Pirates back to good health.

Having earlier been with Orlando Pirates in the guise of a lawyer, Khoza was not with the club when he showed interest in taking over Sundowns. He had first joined Pirates in 1972, after his friend, China 'Dibaba' Hlongwane, recruited him to the club. At the time, Pirates had needed someone who was both intelligent and street-smart (a 'clever', as they put it) to become Pirates' lawyer, and Dibaba decided that his friend, Khoza, could do the job. So Khoza joined the club as a 'lawyer' and was never caught out. But he had to leave the club, fearing for his life, when there was talk of turning Pirates into a company. He has been coy about the real reasons he left and how this was related to the issue of privatising Pirates. One thing that is for sure is that he had dreams of running the club one day. Pirates was a big brand that was also playing a political role in South Africa, with money from some of its matches being used to fund the ANC. He wanted to be the man behind it.

There were divisions in Orlando Pirates, though, and the club did not do so well after Khoza left. But he was still there in the shadows, biding his time and helping the club financially. Why was he interested in Sundowns? Maybe it was that he wanted to save Mahobe's team. Maybe it was greed. Maybe it was just desperation to run a club.

Mahobe would probably have preferred Khoza to buy Sundowns. Maybe they could have struck a deal and still kept him as a shareholder. Khoza and Mahobe were connected by their love for Orlando Pirates and by both being from Soweto. But it was good for both Orlando Pirates and Sundowns that Khoza decided not to pursue the deal. The Krok brothers and the Tsichlases were just what Sundowns needed at the time, and Pirates needed Khoza.

* * *

Anastasia (Natasha) Tsichlas, popularly known as 'The Iron Lady' because of her relentless efforts to keep Sundowns on top, had come with her family to South Africa from Greece. Soccer was not new to her. She started her career in soccer as a secretary at Moroka Swallows in the 1980s and became the matriarch of her soccer-loving family. The man who was to become her husband, Angelo, was a former goalkeeper for Greek side Atromitos, where Natasha's late father had been a board member and chairperson. As fate would have it, they met again at Corinthians, a South African NFL side based in Bedfordview, Johannesburg, and Cupid's arrow struck. Angelo later worked as assistant coach to Mario Tuani at Moroka Swallows, where Natasha worked. He then moved on to coach Blackpool FC.

Angelo, Natasha, and the Krok brothers – who ran the Twin Pharmaceutical Group – formed a company and bought 100 per cent of the club. According to Standard Bank, in February 1989 they bought the club for R400 000 and pledged to invest R1,5 million in it over the next three years, with the aim of 'making Sundowns the biggest club in the country'. The Krok brothers were the majority shareholder, with 51 per cent of the shares, and the Tsichlases owned the remaining 49 per cent. The Twin Pharmaceutical Group became their sponsor. The club dropped 'Mamelodi' from its name and became known simply as Sundowns.

After taking over, the Tsichlases and the Kroks appointed Stan Lapot as head coach and Trott Moloto as assistant. But as Sundowns started losing games, the fans made it clear that they were not happy with Lapot and called for the return of Tshabalala. The management took heed and Tshabalala was brought back as head coach in 1990, again with Moloto as his assistant.

With Screamer at the helm again, Sundowns won the BP Top 8 tournament, the Ohlsson's Champ of Champs Challenge, and the Castle League Championship. But the revival was short-lived, and the 1991 season saw them choking and spluttering, unable to defend the BP Top 8 or the Ohlsson's Champ of Champs Challenge. This led to Tshabalala being fired and replaced by former Peruvian World Cup player Augusto Palacios.

* * *

True to their vision, the new owners of Sundowns were determined to keep the club on top and keep Mahobe's vision alive. The players missed him and all the perks that had come with him being 'the boss', but they still had a healthy Sundowns that was winning games and paying good salaries.

Natasha had a lot of love for Mahobe and acknowledged him as the father of the club that she had taken over. When Sundowns won the Castle League title in 1988, they took the trophy to Sun City Prison to show him.

Notable Sundowns players during Natasha's era included Themba Mnguni, Sizwe Motaung, Lovers Mohlala, Isaac Shai, Matthew Booth, Mark Anderson, John Tlale, Ronny Kananelo (Namibian), Roger De Sa, Roger 'The General' Fetumba (Cameroonian), Linda 'Mercedes Benz' Buthelezi, Zane Moosa, Alex Bapela, Raphael 'Chukwu Train' Chukwu, Eric 'Tambai' Ramasike, Daniel 'Mambush' Mudau, Joel 'Fire' Masilela, Charles Motlohi, Godfrey Sapula, Gift Kampamba (Zambian), Bennet Masinga, Philemon Masinga, Bennet Mnguni, Muisi Ajao (Nigerian), and Augustine Makalakalane.

It was Natasha who brought Raphael Chukwu and Roger Fetumba to Sundowns. Chukwu was a deadly striker, but it was Fetumba, the midfielder, who was a marvel to watch. Most of Sundowns' strikers' goals came courtesy of accurate passes from Fetumba. He was nicknamed 'The General' because he was the man who conducted the symphony from the middle of the pitch; silky and calm, and with a left foot that was marvellously precise in executing instructions from the brain. It was a joy to watch him carve open the opposition teams, creating chance after chance. The fans loved him. A 2014 local publication declared him the greatest player of the PSL era.

There is an interesting story about how Roger Fetumba came to join Sundowns. The Cameroon national team was in South Africa to play Bafana Bafana for the Nelson Mandela Challenge. The game was at King's Park Rugby Stadium in Durban. According to Natasha, she and Angelo sat at opposite ends of the stadium, as they often did when watching soccer, so that they could get different views of the game and later discuss the performances of the players and teams. She was so impressed with Fetumba that she could not wait for the game to end before discussing him. So she called Angelo and found that he had been equally impressed, though somewhat frustrated at sitting there helplessly while the Cameroonian gave the local boys a roasting.

After the game, she stormed into the Cameroonian dressing room, demanding to see Fetumba and insisting that she was not leaving until she had seen him. She was afraid that if she left it for the following day, someone else might talk to him before she did. They agreed in principle that he would join Sundowns, pending formalities.

Natasha's time at the club saw many successes. The period brought the club's first league title, in 1988, with two more following in 1990 and 1993. They followed this up with three consecutive league titles from 1998 to 2000, under the newly formed PSL. Another highlight was reaching the final of the CAF Champions League in 2001, losing 4–1 on aggregate to Egyptian giants Al Ahly.

The bid to get 'Mr Cool' out

– *Makadedelwe!*

As the curtain fell on Mahobe's glamorous life and years of prison lay ahead, his friends were still refusing to make peace with it. They had tried Mangconde's divine intervention, used Khoza's muthi-anointed eggs, and hired the best lawyers, but to no avail. There had to be something else; they racked their brains. Then someone mentioned a man who might be able to help them: CK Motlana. CK, also sometimes known as Oupa, was a man who could fix mysterious problems and make impossible things happen. They decided to approach him.

CK had a home in Dube, Soweto, but he lived in various places, mainly in hotels or with some of his connections in the White suburbs. He only went to live in Soweto when he was low on cash or hiding from someone. He was the go-to man for those in the township wanting to partner with White businessmen, those looking for serious buyers for illegal diamonds and gold, and those seeking favours from high places. He was a man who made things happen. He was also known to be a man of discerning taste, who held his meetings at top hotels and posh restaurants and never spared his clients when it came to his fees. But he had a reputation for delivering the goods. If anyone could pull something out of the hat to save Mahobe, it was him. They arranged to meet with him at the Carlton Hotel in the city centre.

CK listened intently to their problem, hardly interrupting and hardly taking a sip of his drink. Then he gazed at them pensively, one after the other, but did not say anything. There was worry in the eyes of Mahobe's friends; CK was their last hope.

'Gentlemen, I understand your problem and I must say it is quite a unique and complex one,' he said in his trademark British accent. As far as anyone knew, he had not been to the Queen's country to learn her accent, but he spoke it masterfully. They were sitting in the lounge, dressed in their finest suits, and sipping on single malt whisky. They went all out to give CK the impression that they were to be taken seriously. 'It will require pulling strings at the highest levels of government to get your man out of prison. It's going to be costly.'

'We know that, but can it be done?' asked one of Mahobe's friends.

'Yes, it can be done; with the right amount of money, nothing is impossible.'

'Please, my brother, don't just give us false hope.'

'You would not be here if you did not think I could do it. As I said, anything is possible with the right money.'

'How much are we talking?'

He pulled a piece of paper and a pen from his document bag and wrote the amount on the piece of paper and handed it to them. They passed it around for everyone to see. Then they looked at each other, all wanting to say something, but nobody did.

'Guys, we need to talk in private,' said one of them. 'Can you give us a little moment, CK? We need to discuss this.'

'By all means, gentlemen, take all the time you need. I will be at the bar. Just signal me when you're done.'

'It's a lot of money,' said one of the friends once CK was out of range.

'It's madness,' said another. 'But what choice do we have?'

'Guys, do you think this guy can pull it off? It will be a miracle if he does. This is big,' said another.

'Well, you heard what he said. We came to him because we believe that he can do it. He's right. We will just have to trust him. If anyone can do this, it's CK. He is very well connected.'

'Then it's agreed. We'll give him what he has asked.'

With that they signalled him to come back to rejoin them.

'We have discussed your fee and we are all happy with it.'

'Then as soon as I receive the deposit,' said CK, 'I will get on with it. I look forward to doing business with you gentlemen.'

This was great news to Mahobe's friends – a little ray of hope. His fee was divided into two parts: half was to be paid upfront, and the remainder after Mahobe's release from prison. The money was paid by one of Mahobe's close friends who he had helped set up his businesses.

*   *   *

CK was wily as a fox; street-smart, and yet not part of the streets. He was like a chameleon who could adapt himself to any level of South Africa's layered society. He could throw a 'top of the morning' to an Irishman or a disarming *'aangename kennis'* to an Afrikaner. His tongue oozed diplomatic ease. He spoke fluent English (albeit with a fake accent), Afrikaans, seSotho, seTswana, sePedi, isiZulu, and isiXhosa.

CK never wore jeans – they cramped his style. He liked to wear expensive suits, a tie, and a Dobbs hat, and he carried a beautiful walking stick with a brass handle. Outside the township he used to tell people that he was a diplomat from Botswana, which was a former British protectorate.

It was unclear whether Motlana was CK's real surname, but he had managed to cultivate an image of being related to Dr Nthato Motlana, who was a well-respected Sowetan. Dr Motlana was a former Secretary General of the ANC. He was also known for having been the family doctor of Walter Sisulu, Desmond Tutu and Nelson Mandela. During the State of Emergency in 1986, he was part of the Soweto Parents Education Crisis Committee, which was a mechanism for articulating the students' views, applying damage control, and engaging with the government. This image worked well for CK.

He started by arranging a visit to Barberton Prison, where Mahobe was serving his sentence. For the trip, Mahobe's friends hired five Mercedes-Benzes and they drove in a convoy to Barberton. These were CK's instructions. They were all wearing their best suits. The Mercedes that CK was travelling in was in the middle, with two in front and two behind.

As they drove through Benoni, police vehicles appeared out of nowhere and flagged them to stop. They were Afrikaner police. Afrikaner police were always bad news in those days. They looked for any opportunity to either harass or physically harm Black people, especially if such an opportunity arose away from the prying eyes of onlookers. They ordered them out of the cars, but CK was out in a flash and told them to stay put. They were confused but did as he had asked. He then walked towards the police, swinging his trademark stick. He started talking to them, pointing this way and that with his stick as he did so; it was more of a friendly talk than an argumentative one. Next thing, there was a burst of laughter. As he walked back, he told them that everything was under control. 'The police didn't know who I was,' he told them, making sure the police could hear him. 'But everything has been sorted. They are going to escort us out of Benoni.'

When they got out of Benoni, there were other police waiting to escort them to Barberton. It was unheard of for White Afrikaner police to escort a group of Blacks.

CK had told the police that he was a diplomat from Botswana on his way to visit an important prisoner, Zola Mahobe, in Barberton Prison, and they believed him. He had produced his fake Botswana diplomatic passport with all the right stamps. Everybody knew that Mahobe had spent time in Botswana while on the run, so it didn't seem odd that someone from Botswana would want to talk to him. The five Mercedes-Benzes were also spectacle enough to convince anyone that indeed it was someone of very high standing being escorted. Mahobe's friends had a good feeling that CK was going to pull it off. He was certainly putting on a good show.

All eyes were on the five Mercedes-Benzes as they drove through the security gates of Barberton Prison. As soon as the cars stopped, CK was again out in a flash and already talking to some prison warders and pointing with his stick while the rest of the guys remained seated in the cars. Then he motioned them to come out. They were escorted to a private room – an office – which was hastily converted into a visitor's room to accommodate them. They were a sight to behold, in their expensive suits. Everyone – prisoners and warders alike – wanted to get a glimpse of them. Even the head of the prison joined them briefly.

According to Mahlaba, a message had already been sent to the prison warders at Barberton that a diplomat from Botswana was on his way to come and see Mahobe. The calls had apparently come from Pretoria. Whether CK was indeed in cahoots with government officials or whether it was all secretly arranged by him, nobody knew. What everybody wanted to believe was that he was going to succeed in getting Mahobe released.

* * *

CK had the warders hooked on everything he said, both Black and Afrikaner. There was laughter galore in the room, as he cracked jokes about Seretse Khama and his encounters with him. As he continued talking, three warders walked into the room carrying bulging plastic shopping bags. A table was quickly arranged and cake, biscuits, and cold drinks were served. CK never stopped talking.

Then Mahobe was let out of the cell and he came to join them. He was as impressed as the warders at the sight that met his eyes. Of course, CK stood out in his hat and walking stick.

As soon as he walked in, CK went to meet him and gave him a hug. 'This is a very important man,' he said to all those in the room. 'You must treat him with respect.'

'Don't worry, sir. We know who he is; we always treat him with respect,' said one of the Black warders.

'It is good to hear that. Mr Mahobe, you can greet your friends.'

Then Mahobe gave each one of his friends a friendly hug and exchanged a few words before sitting down. Looking at the whole atmosphere – the refreshments, how respectful the warders were being, the way CK carried himself, and the stories from the guys about being escorted by Afrikaner police, Mahobe was also convinced that CK could make the impossible possible.

'Gentlemen, I would like to have a few words in private with Mr Mahobe and his friends, if you don't mind,' he said to the warders.

'It was good talking to you, Mr Motlana,' said one of the warders. 'Take all the time you need. We will just have one warder posted outside the door. I hope you understand.'

'I fully understand. Much appreciated.'

And with that all the warders left the room.

'I'm sure the guys have already told you why I am here,' said CK to Mahobe.

'Yes, they've told me. Are you sure you can pull this off, my brother?'

'All things are possible if you have faith,' said CK with an enigmatic smile. 'Look at this magnificent delegation of ours. Are we not already halfway out the door with you?

Mahobe gave a laugh and relaxed into his chair. 'I can see you have a plan,' he said. 'Just don't get my hopes up. This place is terrible.'

'Don't worry,' said CK. 'You can leave whenever you want to. But there is one condition.'

'And that is?'

'Nobody can know you've been released. That means you have to leave the country. If word gets out that you've escaped, my contacts will get the chop. Is that a deal?'

'I don't have a problem skipping the country straight from here,' said Mahobe. 'I have connections in Zimbabwe – I'll go there.'

'Good choice,' said CK. 'Lesotho, Botswana, Namibia and Swaziland are out. They know too much about you there.'

'Then the problem is solved.'

'Yes, the problem is solved.'

'So what happens next? When do I get out?'

'It is going to take a while. Give me a month to talk to my people and make arrangements. Then your release papers will be prepared and you'll be out of here.'

'My brother, you are a godsend. When you get me out of here, I'm going to add another R50 000 to your fee, I insist.'

'Don't worry,' said CK with a wide grin. 'I'll get you out of here like magic.'

* * *

As the day that CK had promised to get Mahobe released drew near, there was excitement among his friends. They had planned a small private party for him at the home of one of his friends in Pietersburg (now Polokwane). He was to spend one day there and then continue to Zimbabwe the following day.

On the day, they again went to hire Mercedes-Benzes to fetch Mahobe from prison, and everybody was looking forward to a good party that evening. But CK was a no-show. He had just disappeared.

'I told you he couldn't do it,' said one of Mahobe's friends. 'The guy is a bloody con.'

'A bloody good one too; I had so much faith in him,' said another.

'He must give the money back.'

CK was back in Dube a month later, full of excuses about how the release papers had been delayed and how he was still going to get Mahobe released. But Mahobe's friends knew they had been conned. He couldn't explain why he had just disappeared. They had known all along that what he was promising was too good to be true, but they had refused to acknowledge it, blinded by their desire for hope.

Soweto was not short of bold cons and fraudsters. There were those who lived easy on cheque fraud and would find someone inside big companies who could steal a cheque book and copies of the owner's signature. They would then wake up early in the morning, put on their best clothes and hit the road, going from place to place and bank to bank cashing the fraudulent cheques. These were bold men and women who would have to stand in front of the tellers, heart thumping, while the cheques were processed. They knew there was a chance they would be caught out. If a bank thought someone was trying to cash a fraudulent cheque, they would pretend to be taking a long time to process the cheque, but they would just be stalling until the police arrived. The fraudsters would then be arrested on the spot. There were also some, like CK, who conned businessmen eyeing big deals. And then there were the bogus muthi men, prophets and preachers who sold all sorts of miracles to people desperate for hope. It was still as it had been in Sophiatown, only taken to a higher level to go with the times.

In Barberton Prison
– Is'boshwa siphenduka i-Islam

While soccer fans continued to sing his praises and lionise him, Mahobe was entering a new world. Being talked about had once been music to his ears, but now that was a lifetime ago. It is true what they say, that when days are dark, friends are few. One by one, those close to him found a place behind the darkness to hide. Most of them had financially benefited from him in some way – be it in the form of houses, luxury cars, cash injections into their businesses or incomes, or even running those businesses of his that had survived the chop. What if their association with him got Standard Bank sniffing around? What if it decided to extend its investigations to include them? One by one, they vanished into the darkness.

Prison is either a tomb or a womb, they say. Either a man allows bitterness to rot his soul, or he uses the time to quiet his rage and prepare for a rebirth. Desperation was killing Mahobe. More than that, he often found himself confused about whether what he had done was right or wrong. Would he do it again if he were to get another chance? He thought of Snowy a lot. Had it been worth involving her and putting her through all this trauma? She was now in prison for her undying love and loyalty towards him. He missed her dearly.

Even though in prison he was surrounded by people who admired and adored him and regarded him as a victim of apartheid rather than a criminal, he was lonely. He had no one to open up to. There were things he wanted to say to someone, but there was nobody out there. '*Ukuphi, Nkulunkulu wami?*' he whispered to himself, 'Where are you, my God?' He was sitting alone, some distance away from the other prisoners. They were in the physical recreation area of the prison. In Barberton Prison, most prisoners had access to some form of physical recreation at least once a week. He always sat there alone each time they came to the recreational area. 'Hola, Sandawana,' other prisoners would greet him, and then walk past. Everyone knew better than to sit with him.

'Where are you, my God, when I need you?' he whispered to himself again.

Then, as if in answer, someone greeted him. '*As salamu alaikum,*' said the man, appearing from nowhere. 'Do you know me? I am Salim,' he said, taking a seat next to him.

'Did I ask for company? What was that you said?' said Mahobe.

'I come in peace, my brother. *As salamu alaikum*. That's what it means. Peace be upon you.'

Mahobe just nodded. He wished the man would go away.

'So you're the great Zola Mahobe,' said Salim. 'And here you are, in the tjoekie with all us skelms.' Salim chuckled.

Mahobe was silent.

'I've always been a Sundowns fan, did you know that?' said Salim. 'Ever since the days in Marabastad. I know all about the team and I know about you, Zola Mahobe. I know why you ended up here.'

'I ended up here because I tried to make people happy. I was flying high, then I was cut down. I was meant to be a king, not this poor man locked away with criminals.'

'May God have mercy on you,' said Salim. 'The riches that you speak of are not your life any more; they were just a passing phase to real wealth. If the intentions of your crime were to do good to mankind, then Allah will bless you. I cannot judge; only Allah can judge you.'

'What are you? A preacher or something?'

Ignoring him, Salim continued: 'Thank Allah for revealing to you so much sadness, for your happiness will be multiplied. If you give your heart to Allah, you will soon realise that happiness is measured in the units of sadness, and likewise sadness in the units of happiness. The more sadness you know, the more happiness you will know, and likewise the more happiness you know, the more sadness you will know. That is the way of life.'

'Now I am beginning to believe that you are indeed a preacher. Anyway, how come you are here in prison and saying all these things?'

'Many people toil for wealth, thinking that it will bring them happiness,' said Salim, again ignoring his question. 'They are enslaved to money. The more they have, the more they want. Their hearts are never satisfied. They think they want money, but they really want love.'

'Eish, now you're going too far,' said Mahobe. 'And why are you talking about love, Mr Salim? Are you a preacher who fell on the wrong side of life? Are you trying to repent?'

'I'm neither a criminal nor a preacher. I am just a believer.'

'Then how come you are in here in this hole?'

'It is a long story.'

'I have all the time in the world. I might as well listen to your story.'

'Ok,' said Salim. 'I'm originally from Durban, and there is this time when I decided to visit my uncle in Laudium, near Pretoria. During the time I was there, a crime was committed somewhere close to Laudium.'

'Are you talking about the Indian woman whose husband ordered a hit on her to collect on her life insurance?'

'That's the one. The doctor was a gambler and was having financial problems. He decided to take out a life insurance policy on his wife, and a few months later arranged for her to be killed. It was claimed that the murder was committed by two hitmen from Durban.'

'I remember that story,' said Mahobe. 'The media did not report much about it afterwards. But what does that have to do with you?'

'I was identified as one of the hitmen.'

'What? Then how can you say that you are not a criminal? Hitmen are criminals. Killing a person is a crime.'

'It is true, I am not. When I arrived back in Durban after visiting my uncle, the police came to my house and arrested me. I had left Durban to go to Laudium; the murder was committed while I was there; and afterwards I left for Durban. I was mistakenly identified as one of the hitmen.'

'But they can't just pin a murder on you that you didn't commit.'

'Well, the evidence pointed to me. The car driven by the killers was the same model and colour as mine and also had Durban registration plates. The gun used by the killers was also my gun, which I had reported stolen months before, but they believed that I reported it stolen so that I could use it later without taking the blame. They are wrong, of course. Someone who was driving a car that looks like mine and used my stolen gun – the real killer – is out there enjoying freedom, while I am cooped up in here and paying for his crime. I have a strong feeling it is someone who knows me; someone who broke into my house and stole my gun and knew the car that I drove.'

Mahobe shook his head. 'I was sitting here feeling sorry for myself, but now I feel sorry for you.' All of a sudden he felt his problems become lighter, until they became non-problems. He knew what he was in for, and that he deserved it. But this man had found himself serving time for a crime he did not commit. How selfish he had been, to wallow in misery for being in prison for a crime that he had committed; how ungrateful he had been that, despite it all, society still loved him and thought of him as a hero. Everybody out there hated Salim. They wanted him to rot in jail, even though he was innocent.

'Bad things happen to good people and good things happen to bad people,' said Salim. 'It is the way of life and we must accept it. But in the end, Allah will surely make evident the truth, and He will make evident the lies.'

'So what are you doing about it?' asked Mahobe. 'Are you just going to sit there and wait for Allah? You can't let yourself rot in here for a crime you didn't commit.'

'You can't speak like that about Allah, may He forgive you. It's blasphemy. Anyway, I am doing something about it. I have people working on it.'

That evening Mahobe found it hard to sleep. He tossed and turned all night. Here he was, wallowing in sorrow and thinking that he was the saddest man on earth, and there was Salim. Salim had much more reason to be sad. His wife and children were out there being shunned by society. How painful it must be for them. How painful it must be for him.

'My wife and children are beginning to think that I did it,' said Salim when they met again. 'They are beginning to hate me for what I am making them go through. I don't blame them.'

'But they still visit you,' said Mahobe.

'Yes, they still visit me, but I can see it in their eyes; they don't trust me.'

'That must be very hard for you.'

'It is very hard. But as I said, in the end, Allah will make evident the truth and also the lies.'

The conversation with Salim seemed to have taken the weight off his shoulders. He wanted to help. How could a man be so strong in the face of such misery? Where did he get the strength to care for others, when he should be the one seeking pity?

* * *

The following week they met again in the recreation area. Salim was holding a book in his hand.

'*As salamu alaikum wa rahmatullah wa barakatuhu,*' he said, 'May the mercy, peace and blessings of Allah be upon you.'

'God's peace be upon you.'

'No, that's not how you respond to a greeting. You respond by saying "*Wa alaikumus salam wa rahmatullahi wa barakatuhu*", which means "and may the peace, mercy, and blessings of Allah be upon you, too".'

'I am learning.'

'And you are learning well.'

'I have been thinking about what you said. It has made me see a lot that I was not seeing. It is like a weight has been lifted off my shoulders.'

'I have been thinking about you, too,' said Salim, 'and I decided to get you this.'

'What is it? I am not much of a reader.'

'Then read it slowly. It is a holy book, after all.'

Mahobe took the book and opened it. 'Is this the Quran?'

'Yes, you are lucky I found you an English version. Read a little bit every day, and your life will change.'

'As I said, I am not much of a reader, but I'll try.'

'That's good enough, my friend.'

'And what about your case; how good are these people who are working on it? I would like to help if you'll let me.'

'How can you possibly help me from inside here? What I need is someone who can track down the real killers. Then the truth will come out and I can get out of here.'

'You said yourself that in the end, Allah will make evident those who are truthful and those who are not. I know people who know people who know people, if you know what I mean. I can help you track down the murderers.'

'*Insha Allah*,' he said, 'if God is willing.'

'Just give me a chance and let's see how it goes. It's worth a try. It can't do any harm.'

'May Allah reward you with good.'

'Then it's settled.'

It felt good that Salim had allowed him to help. It was as if he was giving him a chance to repent, to show appreciation for life and to contribute to its greater meaning.

Later, when Mahobe sat in his cell reading the Quran, he found a folded piece of paper between two pages. He opened it and found a handwritten message: *Dear friend. Always remember: When Allah has shown you the way there is nothing to stop you from getting there. To be afraid and to cast a doubt is to build a bed of thorns where you shall lie.*

Which way had God shown him? He had lost his dear soccer team and there was hollowness inside him. He was separated from his soulmate, Snowy, and he had no one to open up to. Was there a purpose in all of this? What was Salim telling him? He had prayed to God not knowing what he was praying for. Was it to get out of prison? Was that what he prayed for? If he were to get out of prison, then what? He could certainly not go back to the life he had lived – that was in the past. He had vowed that he was going to buy back Sundowns, but was that what he really yearned for? Was he stuck in the past, pitying himself and crying over that which he could not get back, instead of looking into the future? What future?

* * *

He started reading the Quran with eagerness. He wanted to discover where Salim got his strength from; the strength that made him stand so tall and unshakable, even in a storm of hatred and resentment; the strength that had its source in the hidden depths of the soul. Was Salim destined for greater happiness? Was that the reason why his soul was tormented so? 'Thank Allah for revealing to you so much sadness, for your happiness will be multiplied,' he remembered him saying.

He loved the Quran, but found it hard to yield to its teachings. There were parts of it that talked to his soul and parts that did not. 'Why are religions so complicated?' The words came out of his mouth unbidden. Did it make him an unbeliever, that it was so difficult for him to believe in that which he could not comprehend?

'Do you think that I will ever be a true believer?' he asked Salim the next time they met. The other prisoners had stopped greeting them because each time they went past, Mahobe and Salim would be in deep conversation and ignored their greetings.

'Why are you asking whether you will ever be a true believer?'

'Because there are some things in the Quran that I cannot comprehend. I'm all for the message of peace and love and loving my neighbour as I love myself, but there are certain sayings that I don't get. For instance, I cannot comprehend the day of judgement to come. I believe the day of judgement is in our lifetime, and that when we die, we leave our bodies and exist in spirit – in the minds of people. Eternal life, to me, is finding a place to rest in the minds and spirits of people, and those who find it are those who have made a lasting impression on mankind.'

'It's good that you have opened up to me about this. The messenger of Allah, *Sallallahu Alaihi Wasallam*, says leave that which makes you doubt. Concentrate on the parts that do not bring doubt into your mind first, and more will be revealed to you. Allah will guide you into the light.'

* * *

Stix came to visit Mahobe in prison, and they agreed that he would look into Salim's matter and try to track down the real killers. It was not going to be an easy job, especially because the public and the few witnesses who had caught a glimpse of the car used in the hit and of its occupants all thought that Salim was one of the hitmen. He had vehemently denied any involvement, but the state and the public had concluded that he was just protecting the other hitman. Stix had his work cut out.

'Was salamu alaikumus wa rahmatullah wa barakatuhu,' said Salim. They were again in the recreation area.

'Wa alaikumus salam wa rahmatullah wa barakatuhu,' replied Mahobe. 'I had a visit from a dear friend of mine and I raised your matter with him. He's on it as we speak. Soon we will find out who the real killers are.'

'Actually, I wanted to talk to you about that,' said Salim. 'My people have found a lead. The killers are indeed from Durban. It seems the spirit of the doctor's wife would not stop haunting him. He has come forward and made a confession, praise be to Allah.'

'Alhamdulillah! So now the real truth is going to come out?'

'It is the will of Allah. Finally, my name can be removed from the book of the darkness. I am glad that this burden will be lifted off my wife and children's shoulders. They have suffered enough.'

'So what is going to happen now?'

'Now my lawyers are working to get me out of here. It is just a formality. The doctor has named the hitmen and one of them has already been arrested. One is still on the run. The one arrested will appear in court soon; then my name will be cleared.'

A weight had been removed from Mahobe's shoulders. He was happy for Salim.

'I can't wait to be out of here. I can't wait to be with my family again.'

'I am happy for you,' said Mahobe. 'As for me, I deserve to be in here.'

'Just think of it this way: you did not harm anyone.'

'No, I harmed someone. I harmed my partner. I harmed my Snowy. She should not have gone to jail. I have destroyed her life.'

'No, you have not. Allah is with her. From what you have told me of her, she is a good person. She will also see the glory of Allah. Our mistakes do not destroy us but help us to see the bigger purpose to living. Believe me, she is a different person now.'

'I am going to miss you.'

'I will visit often, my friend.'

In less than a month, the formalities were over and Salim's release papers had been prepared.

'You must keep your promise to visit,' said Mahobe as Salim prepared to walk out of the prison gate.

'I promise you I will visit as often as I can.'

'May Allah watch over you.'

'May He watch over you, too. Keep reading the Quran. You will find inner happiness.'

* * *

It was not long before Salim came to visit. He was with someone else.

'This is Bilal, the spiritual leader in my community.'

'*As salamu alaikum wa rahmatullah wa barakatuhu,*' said Bilal.

'*Wa alaikum salam wa rahmatullah wa barakatuhu,*' said Mahobe.

'Bilal is here to help you with any questions you might have about Islam,' said Salim.

'It is actually a good thing that you brought him along,' said Mahobe. 'I've made a lot of progress with my reading and, to tell you the truth, I like what I am discovering. You were right that things would slowly be revealed to me. I now know I want to follow the teachings of Islam,' he said.

'This is the greatest news I have heard in a long time,' said Salim.

'Great news, indeed,' said Bilal. '*Barakah Allah.*'

'It is an easy process converting to Islam,' he continued. 'But you will have to be sure that this is what you want. You will have to completely submit to Allah.'

'My mind is made up,' said Mahobe.

'I am glad to hear that. Salim has already taught you a lot about Islam, but there is more.'

'I am ready for it. Allah will give me strength.'

'Cleanliness is a big part of Islam,' said Bilal. 'You must bathe at least once a day and do ritual washing before prayers.' Bilal proceeded to give him a list of cleanliness tasks, from brushing his teeth to keeping his clothes neat and clean. 'You must respect others and help others in need,' continued Bilal. 'You must do good deeds. Praying and fasting helps. You must also keep your surroundings clean. I know it sounds like a long list of requirements.'

'It is not a big ask; it makes sense. I will abide.'

'Please repeat after me. *I bear witness that no one deserves to be worshipped except Allah, and I bear witness that Muhammad is the last Messenger of Allah.*'

Mahobe repeated the words.

'You are now our new brother,' said Bilal. 'We will be with you every step of the way.'

Release from prison
– Indodana yolahleko

Five long, lonely, mundane, violent and hopeless years passed slowly for Mahobe before he became eligible for parole. But there was a hurdle to overcome – Standard Bank had decided to oppose his parole. The institution wrote formally to the Ministry of Justice, pointing out that releasing Mahobe on parole would send the wrong message to the community at large. But to his delight, the challenge failed, and he was granted parole.

As the day of his release drew nearer, he found himself thinking more and more about what kind of life awaited him out there. He still had a home and he still had Snowy. What was it going to be like, being reunited with her? The last time they had touched each other was the day before he had departed for the Bush Bucks match in Durban, way back in May 1987. It was about six years ago. Did he still love her? He had not thought about that. He had been so engrossed in the Quran that the thought had hardly crossed his mind. Of course he loved her; he had always loved her. But that was in their past life. He had changed and she had changed. Prison is a tomb or a womb. How had she changed? Had she died out there in prison, or had she been reborn? Who had she become in her rebirth?

His thoughts drifted to Sundowns and its fans, and he wondered how they were going to react to the news of his release. He knew that they loved him; they would always love him. Sundowns was his baby; his and Snowy's. He felt like a father whose child had been taken away from him, to be raised by another man and his wife. The irony of it was that Sundowns was indeed being raised by another man and his wife – the Tsichlases – and they were taking good care of it. The baby was doing well – *Alhamdulillah*.

He was determined to make it out there. He had inner strength, and the time had come to put it to the test. He still had a few businesses being run by some of his friends. But could he trust them? They had never come to visit him in prison. They wanted no association with him. They had all found shelter in the darkness, the darkness that he could no longer penetrate. He was now in the light and had no desire for the darkness. He still had Snowy; he still had his brother; he still had his children. And he still had Six Morake and Stix. He had so much to look forward to.

As the day of his release drew near, he asked for the clothes that he had been wearing the day he was arrested in Botswana – the tracksuit and running shoes – to be burned. It was a ritual of death and rebirth. He was a different person now, no longer the same man who was arrested on that fateful morning of 27 January 1988. He asked for brand-new clothes to wear when he got out. It was a new world, a new life, a new beginning.

Snowy, Stix, and two other friends came to fetch him from prison. There was no fanfare to herald his release, no journalists to cover the story, no crowds waiting to greet him. Out of sight, out of mind, they say. It was just the way he had wished it. He did not want the media hovering around or any spectacle made of his release. He wore a beautiful Muslim outfit of a long white shirt, white trousers, white shoes and a white taqiyah cap with a thin band of green and yellow, the colours of Sundowns.

Also waiting for him outside the prison were Salim and Bilal.

'As salamu alaikum wa rahmatullah wa barakatuhu,' said Salim.

'Wa alaikum salam wa rahmatullah wa barakatuhu,' said Mahobe. 'You remembered!'

'How could I forget, my friend?' Salim said as they embraced.

Mahobe turned to Snowy. 'My love, these are the people who made my life bearable in prison. Come and meet them.'

* * *

The sun shone brightly and there wasn't a cloud in the sky. He was thankful for freedom, scary though it was. As the car drove through the prison gates, he held Snowy close and kissed her. They sat together in the back seat of the car, which was driven by one of his friends. There were only three of them in the car. He did not speak, and neither did she. It was an agreement made in silence; each was engrossed in their own thoughts and contemplating what the future held in store for them. They were both warm in each other's arms. He felt his spirit lift high up into the sky, floating like angels looking down upon the earthlings. She was there, floating with him.

So much had happened while he had been in prison. It was a brand-new world; a world far removed from the one he had left. President FW de Klerk, the last president of apartheid South Africa, had surprised the world when he announced on

2 February 1990 the imminent release of Nelson Mandela from prison and the unbanning of the ANC, PAC and South African Communist Party. Mandela was released on 11 February. By 1991, legislation had been passed that allowed all races to own property anywhere in the country, and in December of that year, key political leaders began formal constitutional negotiations. The process of ushering in democracy in South Africa was well underway and irreversible.

Many exiles were on their way back home. Mahobe thought of his brother, who had taken up arms to liberate the country. He was also back home. And here he was, also returning home. He felt one with them. He was also returning home from the exile of prison. He had followed the developments while in prison, but he was not a part of them. Here, outside prison, was where it was all happening.

'*Alhamdulillah*,' he said.

'What was that you said, love?' asked Snowy.

'It means praise be to God,' he said. 'It's something I learnt while in prison. It's a long story; a story for another day.'

As they went past a sign that read 'Johannesburg', his spirits were again lifted high. He felt a rush of adrenaline in his veins. He was back in the city of lights, the city where he belonged, where most men with a conscience soon hid it away.

'*Astaghfirullah*,' he said, 'May Allah forgive me'.

'Another something that you learnt in prison?' asked Snowy.

'Yes. There is a lot that I learnt while in prison.'

'There is a lot that I learnt, too. But it's a story for another day.'

Prison had hardened her too.

***

A rich man acquires many friends, but who wants to be with a poor man? Many of his friends had deserted him. They had moved on and had no place for him in their lives now. Some even derided him, referring to him as *lepantiti*, meaning jailbird. These were people who used to eat, drink, and laugh with him; people who at some stage had called him 'friend' and 'brother'. He had helped build the careers of most of them and used to shower them with lavish gifts, like houses and expensive cars. Some spread malicious rumours that he was asking for donations from those who used to be close to him, but it was a lie. Others spread rumours that he could not even afford food, and that he ate spinach and pap for dinner. One day, a distant cousin of his with offices in Sandton promised to lend him money. He made him wait at reception for a long time, and when he finally made an appearance, he was surrounded by a group of his staff members. 'Do you know who this is?' he said to them. 'This is the great Zola Mahobe. He used to be a very rich man, and look at him now.' Then he told him that he could not help him with the money he had promised. Mahobe was stung by their cruelty. But they did not owe him anything.

But those who were still running his businesses did owe him; they at least owed him the money that he had used to set up the businesses. The businesses belonged to him, and were theirs only in name. But crooks are crooks; honesty and loyalty don't exist in their language. Money, on the other hand – now, that's something. 'Just leave this alone, broer,' said one of them. 'You cannot claim to own a business that you left over six years ago. I could have left it to die. I don't owe you. Besides, you have no proof.' Some ducked and dived and never made time to meet with him. It was always a bad time to meet. They knew that there was nothing he could do, short of exposing the fact that he had not disclosed everything that he owned during his court trial. His hands were tied. Reality started to sink in. How could he have been so wrong about them?

His one consolation was the discovery that soccer fans continued to love him the way they had loved him before he went to prison. Soon the whole of South Africa knew that he was out of prison, and Sundowns fans wanted him back at Sundowns playing some role, however small. After all, it was his baby being taken care of by the Tsichlases and the Kroks. But the baby had grown and was healthy and happy with its foster parents.

'Ma-Stix, what would you do if you were me?' he said to his friend. Stix had paid him a visit at his home in Rockville. He was one of the very few friends who came to visit.

'What are you talking about?'

'What would you do if your baby had to be taken away from you to be raised by someone because something happened to you that made you unable to provide for it, and then years later you find yourself in a position where you could take back your baby? Would you try to take it back?'

'That's a difficult one. I guess it would depend on the baby, whether it wants to come back to live with me or whether it is happy living with the foster parents.'

'Let's say that the baby is happy living with its foster parents and it is healthy, and that it loves its foster parents as much as it loves you.'

'I don't know whether I would be able to just look on. I would want to get the baby back, yet I would also not want to upset the foster parents.'

'So what would you do?'

Stix sat thinking for a moment. 'This baby we are talking about, is it one of your many children, or is it perhaps a soccer team?'

'The team,' said Mahobe. 'When I left for prison I vowed to get it back some day, but I don't know any more. So much has changed.'

It was as if the Tsichlases could sense his longing. They listened to the fans who called for him to continue to play some role at Sundowns; to co-parent the baby, so to speak. But it was not only because of the fans that they wanted him back at Sundowns; they knew that it was he who had built the Sundowns brand into what it was. They made him a director at Sundowns. The fans were happy. Journalists started to take interest in him again and even sought his opinion on Sundowns. He was back in the spotlight again, albeit a dimmed one. But that was the way he wanted it. He needed time to gather himself. The Tsichlases had always been good friends, and they would continue to be.

Motsepe takes over Sundowns

– Iphupho le Africa

In 2003, the Krok brothers sold their 51 per cent controlling interest in the club to mining magnate Patrice Motsepe, a well known businessman and the first Black South African to be included on Forbes' annual list of billionaires. A year later, Motsepe bought the remaining 49 per cent share from the Tsichlases for an estimated R65 million and became sole owner and shareholder of the club. The club was renamed Mamelodi Sundowns as a nod to its heritage. Abe Krok remained an honorary chairperson, in appreciation of his role in turning Sundowns into one of the PSL's glamour clubs, alongside Kaizer Chiefs and Orlando Pirates. Natasha and Angelo stayed on at the club as non-executive directors.

Natasha was proud of the work she had done with Sundowns over nearly two decades. She was also glad they had sold to Motsepe. There were other powerful people interested in buying the club at the time, but they chose Motsepe knowing he would continue the legacy. Now Motsepe was taking things to another level at Sundowns, matching the salaries of some overseas teams. The sky continued to be the limit at Sundowns.

Indeed, Sundowns was a very lucky team. It was lucky when it was saved by Dr Motsiri Itsweng, Dr Bonny Sebotsane and Joseph Nchimane 'Fish' Kekana from possible demise way back in 1979, when Ingle Singh and the other owners at the time were struggling to keep the club afloat financially. It was also lucky when Dr Itsweng and company found themselves in financial difficulty and Zola Mahobe stepped in to save it. Sundowns was again in trouble when Mahobe and Snowy's dealings were exposed, but once again the club was lucky when Standard Bank temporarily took over and kept it well and healthy while looking for suitable buyers. Then the Tsichlases and the Krok brothers stepped in, and they took Sundowns to even greater heights, signing some of the best players from South Africa and the continent and paying good salaries. Now, the club was again lucky when Motsepe, whose style in many ways has reminded people of the days of Mahobe, took over full ownership of the club.

As soccer bosses, both Mahobe and Motsepe distinguished themselves by knowing the value of good players and being willing to pay top salaries and buy the best talent. They both poured money from their own pocket into the club, even though, technically, Mahobe's money was never his own. The Mamelodi Sundowns players of today under Motsepe are as happy as those of yesteryear under Mahobe.

In 2016, Sundowns won the CAF Champions League, beating Egyptian giants Zamalek 3–1 on aggregate. Sundowns was only the second South African soccer club to do so, after Orlando Pirates won it in 1995. The prize money was $1,5 million (about R20,9 million). Motsepe was elated – this was a dream come true for him. He decided to give all of the money to the team. He was at the OR Tambo International Airport when he announced that the team would keep all the money. He left it to them to decide how they were going to divide it among themselves. But he had some advice for them: they should not blow it all, but rather invest it. It would support them when their soccer playing days were over, he said.

In May 2018, Motsepe brought Barcelona to South Africa to play against Mamelodi Sundowns. It was history in the making, not only for South African soccer in general, but also for the Sundowns players, who got to rub shoulders with some of the greatest players in the world, such as Iniesta, Lionel Messi, Piqué, Jordi Alba, Vidal, Busquets, and Suárez. It was also a wonderful spectacle for the soccer-loving people of South Africa.

In 2021, Mamelodi Sundowns announced their partnership with a world-renowned sports agency, Roc Nation Sports, which is owned by American business magnate Shawn 'Jay-Z' Carter. The company has a mission to drive change and uplift communities. Roc Nation chose Sundowns because of their inspiring story and their iconic status on the African continent.

Sundowns, under Motsepe, was also the first South African team to win back-to-back matches against Al Ahly, when they beat them 1–0 both home and away in the 2022 CAF Champions League group stages.

The sky continues to be the limit at Mamelodi Sundowns. They continue to be one of the best teams in South Africa, if not the best, and they continue to make their presence felt on the continent.

The curtain falls

– *Kwacisha ukukhanya*

After prison, Mahobe lived with Snowy in Rockville. But prison had changed them. They were no longer looking for the same things in life. Snowy no longer had dreams of fame and fortune. Even though she was only in her thirties, she had decided she had seen it all and just wanted a quiet life, away from the camera lenses and journalists hovering around with their notebooks. But Mahobe was not done yet; he was only 40, and his youthful spirit had not left him.

'You know what, my love; when I went to prison, I vowed that I would get Sundowns back, but I am no longer sure.'

'I think that's a good decision. We had our time in the spotlight, and we should make peace with our lives now.'

'You're right, we should make peace with our lives, especially regarding Sundowns. It's doing well and should be left alone. But I still want to get into soccer big time. It is the one thing that I love the most in my life, apart from you and my loved ones, of course. But I will have to build myself up first.'

'Aren't you ashamed?' asked Snowy.

'Ashamed of what?'

'Of being out there in public again? People are still talking, you know? The less I am seen out there in public the better for me. I don't want to be in the spotlight any more.'

'Perhaps you're still adjusting. We are going to climb to the top again.'

'I am not sure I want to be there again.'

'Just give yourself time.'

But they were drifting apart. Snowy hardly left the house, and Mahobe found himself without her most of the time. There was something separating them, something pushing them in opposite directions. He would go on about his ambitions and schemes to make money, but she was not interested.

'Love, did you hear a thing I said?' was his usual refrain each time he tried to talk to her.

'What was that you were saying? Sorry, I wasn't listening,' she would say, removing the headphones of her Sony Walkman from her ears. Lately, all she did was listen to gospel music on the Walkman. She walked around and did everything in the house wearing her headphones. They would argue about it, but she did not seem to care.

'Snowy, do you still love me?'

'Why are you asking?'

'It's just that you don't seem to be interested in me any more. We don't talk any more, and to tell you the truth it makes me feel very lonely. We don't do things together like we used to.'

'That was in another life. Things have changed. I told you, I am done with the life of fame.'

He just could not get through to her.

Mahobe started spending more time with someone else who made him feel alive again. Her name was Manunu, and he had known her since she was a young girl. He fell in love with her. When he told Snowy it was no surprise to her. 'I am happy for you,' was all she could say. She did not seem to care. She was numb. In her mind, it had ended a long time ago between them. They had not touched each other in a long time. They decided to part ways, and they sold the house in Rockville and split the money. The house was later modified by the new owner, but the street name remained: Mahobe Street. It still remains the one reminder of Mahobe's greatness.

Snowy continued to live a quiet and subdued life at her family home in Orlando East, while Mahobe carried on with Manunu and ultimately married her. They had a child together. That was child number five for Mahobe.

So the curtain fell on the life of Tebello Snowy Moshoeshoe and Zola Daniel Mahobe – sophisticates, lovers, comrades in arms – the Bonnie and Clyde of Soweto, who stole from the privileged to create something that gave joy and hope to the nation.

Snowy Moshoeshoe, the woman who played a maverick role in helping Mahobe to build his empire, succumbed to ovarian cancer on 14 July 2010, at the age of 51. She had only been diagnosed in March of that year, at Unitas Hospital in Centurion. She died a lonely death, forgotten by the world that once upon a time sang her praises.

There was not much media coverage of her passing; just a single article on the internet. It was only three days after the 2010 FIFA World Cup Final when she died, and the news of her passing was overshadowed by that historic goal by the Spanish midfield maestro, Andrés Iniesta, which saw Spain crowned the champions. The 2010 World Cup, which was held in South Africa, was the biggest party the nation had ever seen. Ailing as she was, Snowy had managed to be a part of it and to see that historic moment.

Mourners gathered at her family home in Orlando East described her as a woman who, since coming out of prison, had transformed from the carefree, flamboyant young woman she had been into a nurturing, caring friend who, despite her no-nonsense attitude, put those around her first and cared for their wellbeing. Another mourner described her as one of the few local women in the 1980s who was known for her flashy lifestyle and socialising with the who's who of South African soccer and international dignitaries. South African soccer will be forever grateful for her efforts. True Sundowns fans will never forget her.

Mauser, Mr Cool

– Dloz'lam

'You know what, *ntwana*, I saw you growing up as a little boy but I didn't know you were so trustworthy,' said Mahobe to Sipho Mahlaba. It was late 2013 and they were driving to Cape Town, where Mahobe had been trying to close a business deal. Lately he had been chasing mining deals in gravel quarries and iron ore. It was not clear where he got the money from for these deals, but he had his sources. There were three of them in the car: Mahobe, his younger brother – the one who used to be an APLA man – and Mahlaba.

'Ok, I have always known that I could trust you more than anyone,' he continued. 'What I am saying is that there is no one that I trust more than you right now. I should have left you in charge of my businesses. It did cross my mind, back then when I became a wanted man, but there was no time to think about it. Things happened too fast.'

'You're right, and I don't blame you.'

'Do me a favour, *ntwana*; I want you to bury me when I die. You know I am a Muslim. I want you to bury me in the Muslim tradition. You will explain that to my folks; they don't know much about Islam.'

Mahlaba was taken aback by the mention of death, and so was Mahobe's brother. That was not the kind of talk they had expected. There was nothing wrong with his health – at least that's what they thought.

'What are you talking about? You are not dying,' said Mahlaba.

Mahobe did not reply.

'Don't speak like that. You are beginning to scare me,' added his brother.

They left it at that and continued to Cape Town. Then on their way back, he again told Mahlaba that he would like him to bury him when he died.

'What makes you think that you are going to die before me?' Mahlaba asked him, trying to make light of the conversation. But he was beginning to get worried. 'Maybe I should also ask you to bury me when I die,' he continued.

* * *

Early on the morning of Friday, 13 December 2013, Mahlaba got a call from Mahobe's family saying that Mahobe had just collapsed in the house. He rushed to Mahobe's house as fast as he could. He was confused – Mahobe had not complained of anything the last time they were together. Friday the thirteenth; is it true what they say about it? Is it true that it is a day of bad luck? he kept asking himself. When he got to the house they had called the ambulance and it had already left. He got a few close relatives into his car and followed the ambulance to Baragwanath Hospital. 'Mahobe was not too bad and was talking when he left in the ambulance,' they said.

They arrived at the hospital at around nine in the morning and found Mahobe in a wheelchair, waiting for the doctor. It was an anticlimax. They were hoping for action – frantic action to try to save his life. They tried to impress upon the nurses that they thought his condition was serious and that he required immediate attention, but the nurses just told them to wait. They were frustrated. He was complaining of a sharp pain each time he tried to lift his left arm.

When he realised that help was not going to come anytime soon, Mahobe gave one of the nurses Patrice Motsepe's phone number and asked them to call him, hoping that he would make a plan to move him to a private hospital. He knew that he was not going to make it if he remained at Baragwanath.

It was a desperate time. He was staring death in the eyes – death that could possibly be avoided if only he could get professional attention immediately. It was the worst feeling of helplessness. Nobody knew what had happened with the call to Motsepe, whether he had received it or not, and they waited and waited for the doctor until they had almost given up hope.

The doctor finally arrived and took him for X-rays at about half past two – more than five hours after he had arrived. He was admitted and the family were told they could go home.

The following day, the family was called urgently to the hospital. What they feared the most had happened – Mahobe was no more. He must have known that there was something wrong with him but had decided to keep quiet about it. His brother told the family of his wish to be buried in the Muslim tradition and nobody objected. He was supposed to be buried the same day that he died, but because many of his relatives had not received the message yet, and because they had not been aware of his wish to be buried in the Muslim tradition, it was decided that he would be buried early the following day.

His body was moved to Lens, the local Islamic mortuary. On the morning of Sunday, 15 December, the imams called members of his family to Lens to wash him. They smeared him with oil and perfumes and wrapped him neatly in strips of fine linen. Then he was taken to the graveyard where he was buried.

* * *

It was déjà vu – Sophiatown again. Just as it had rained that whole week leading to his entry into this world, it rained the whole week leading to his exit from it. It was also the week that South Africans bid farewell to Nelson Mandela, the man who many referred to as 'Tata', meaning 'Dad'. Multitudes packed the FNB Stadium, where Mandela's memorial service was held before his funeral. Leaders of the world and international celebrities had converged on South Africa to pay their last respects. Barack Obama, president of the US, was there; Oprah Winfrey was there; David Cameron, prime minister of the UK, was there; and Raul Castro, president of Cuba, was there. There were over a hundred heads of state and many other country representatives at the memorial service.

Mahobe was buried on the same day that Mandela was buried. As South Africans and the people of the world woke up early on that Sunday, 15 December, to switch on their TVs to follow the proceedings in Qunu, where Mandela was being buried, Mahobe was also being buried, at Lens. It had been the same with Snowy's death: that had also been overshadowed by an event of great magnitude, the 2010 FIFA World Cup.

Paying tribute to him at the memorial service organised by Mamelodi Sundowns in Pretoria, Patrice Motsepe said Mahobe had laid the foundation for the development and success of Sundowns. 'His contribution is there, and will be there forever. We will be eternally grateful to Mahobe.'

It may seem that Motsepe was merely being polite, but in truth, Mahobe is remembered by South Africans with admiration, despite his crime. The SABC described his passing as a loss for the South African sports fraternity, and credited him with transforming Sundowns into one of the biggest clubs in the country.

Fondly referred to as Mauser by those at Sundowns who had been close to him, he will remain the number-one man in the eyes and hearts and souls of Sundowns supporters. Alex Shakoane, an official at Mamelodi Sundowns, credited him with changing the face of soccer in South Africa. He was not the only one who felt that way.

Who would have thought that some of the greatest steps forward in South African soccer would have come about as a result of a bank heist?

Actions are judged by intentions

A tribute by Natasha Tsichlas

The story of Mahobe would not be complete without a word from Natasha Tsichlas, a dear friend of his, who continually communicated with him during those turbulent times after he was arrested, and who saw to it that what he had started with Sundowns did not go to waste. 'I must say that Zola Mahobe – he was actually a very kind person,' she said during an interview for this book with Nikolais Kirkinis. Natasha continued:

> He was very clever but also very nice, really down to earth. He never had the arrogance. He was different from other club owners.
>
> He had a lot of businesses, which certain so-called friends took from him after he went to prison. But as a person, he was a good family man. He was good to his children. Unfortunately, after his arrest, his family faced a lot of problems because no one was looking after them. As I said, they took everything from him. Lots of people took opportunities when he was put away, and as a result, his family really did suffer.
>
> Even when he came back from prison, he was still, how do you say? He didn't hold any grudges for nobody. It's very strange, for a person who lost everything to come out still with love in his heart. He still loved Sundowns, very much so. We made him a director of the club later on, and he always wanted to add to the success of the club. He was never a bitter man. I never saw him cross; he was always with a smile – and

very calm. To me, he was really a leader, and no matter what happened, his personality never changed. We were very sad when he left us, and he was too young when he went.

My favourite story with Zola was in 1988, when Angelo and Mario won the league with Sundowns. They decided to go visit Zola in prison, the two of them with the trophy. I couldn't go to the prison, being a woman, but the two of them decided it was important. Zola was crying when they got to the prison. He was so emotional; so thankful. He was so grateful that people still remembered him. Angelo and Mario wanted Zola to touch the trophy, to tell him that it was mainly through his efforts that the club had won the league.

Zola was very influential on Sundowns, even from within prison. When we first took the club, we had problems; there would be people trying to harass us and intimidate us. Zola would send a message from inside, saying that the people must leave us to do our work. 'These people are going to save the club,' he said, 'you must allow them to do their work.' There were a lot of vultures out there, who wanted to dissolve the club, sell off all the players and destroy Sundowns. We wanted to build it. We wanted to build it with Zola's support. And that was the beauty of Zola's personality – he was not jealous. He understood that in order for Sundowns to be saved, we needed to work together. And you can see this club today, where it is, the best club on the continent. What I'm trying to say is, Zola blessed this club, and that is a big reason why it is where it is today.

Characters in the book and past players

Main characters:
Zola Daniel Mahobe (worked: Rank Xerox, IBM, and Standard Bank before starting his first company, Power Promotions)
Snowy Moshoeshoe (Mahobe's girlfriend: worked at Leratong Hospital before joining Standard Bank)
Gladys (worked at Standard Bank)

Mahobe's close friends:
Six Morake
Jabu Mthethwa
Sipho Mahlaba
Stix
Pat
Ace
Mahobe's PAC lady comrade

Mahobe business partners:
Benny Len
Elio Rossi

Mahobe's legal team:
The law firm *Maluleke, Seriti and Moseneke*
(George Maluleke, Willie Seriti, and Dikgang Moseneke).

Magistrate:
Magistrate Booysens

Mahobe's uncle:
Harrison Selulu

Mothers of Mahobe's children:
Mandisa
Manunu
Siza

Characters involved in trying to save Mahobe from prison term:
CK Motlana
Khoza (muthi man)
Mangconde (muthi woman)

Mahobe's Muslim friends:
Bilal
Salim

Soccer bosses before and during Mahobe's time:
Abdul Bhamjee (NPSL and NSL's PRO)
Cyril Kobus (NPSL's general manager)
George Thabe (NPSL)
Kaizer Motaung (Kaizer Chiefs)
Jack 'Big Daddy' Sello (Moroka Swallows)
Jomo Sono (Jomo Cosmos)
Ewert 'The Lip' Nene (Kaizer Chiefs)

The man who played a role that led to the birth of Mamelodi Sundowns:
Boy Mafa

Previous and current owners of Mamelodi Sundowns:
Angelo Tsichlas (Sundowns)
Dr Bonny Sebotsane (Mamelodi Sundowns)
Dr Motsiri Itsweng (Mamelodi Sundowns)
Ingle Singh (Marabastad Sundowns)
Joseph Nchimane 'Fish' Kekana (Mamelodi Sundowns)
Natasha Tsichlas (Sundowns)
Patrice Motsepe Dr. h.c. (Mamelodi Sundowns)
Standard Bank (Mamelodi Sundowns)
The Krok brothers (Sundowns)
Zola Mahobe (Mamelodi Sundowns)

Mamelodi Sundowns captain during and soon after Mohobe's time at the club:
Mike Ntombela

Major players in the formation of NSL:
Abdul Bhamjee
Cyril Kobus
Kaizer Motaung Dr h.c.
Irvin Khoza Dr h.c.

Soccer characters who became victims of the violence of the breakup of the NSL:
Aaron 'Roadblock' Makhathini
China 'Dibaba' Hlongwane

Some notable players that Mahobe's money could not buy:
Johny 'Black Sunday' Masegela
Isaac 'Shakes' Kungwane
Nelson 'Teenage' Dlacla

Past football associations:
Whites-only South African Football Association (SAFA)
Federation Professional League (FPL)
National Professional Soccer League (NPSL)
National Football League (NFL)
South African National Football Association (SANFA)

Some notable South African players playing overseas before and during the 1980s:
Albert 'Hurry-Hurry' Johanneson
Stephen Madi 'The Black Meteor' Mokone,
Gary Bailey
Bruce Grobbelaar

Former Mamelodi Sundowns coaches:
Ben Segale (appointed by Mahobe)
Screamer Tshabalala (appointed by Mahobe and carried on when Standard Bank took over)
Mario Tuani (appointed by Standard Bank)
Augusto Palacios (appointed by Standard Bank)
Stan Lapot (appointed by the Tsichlases)
Screamer Tshabalala (appointed by the Tsichlases)

Interim committee members during Standard Bank's takeover of Mamelodi Sundowns:
Don Macey (Standard Bank)
Willie Seriti
Dr Motsiri Itsweng
Dr Bonny Sebotsane
Ngamula Malewa
Screamer Tshabalala

Some of the notable Mamelodi Sundowns players during the Mahobe era

Ace Khuse
Alpheus Mabusela
Andries 'Panyaza' Chitja
Bashin Mahlangu
Basil Steenkamp
Hamilton Mahlangu
Harold 'Jazzy Queen' Legodi
Harris 'TV4' Tshoeu
Jan 'Malombo' Lechaba
Jeff Nkomo
Johannes 'Bricks' Mudau
John Salter
Lovemore Chafunya
Majesty Mogoboa (masseur)
Mark 'Lesilo' Anderson
Mike 'Nanana' Ntombela
Mike 'Sporo' Mangena
Mike Ndanda
Papi Lekala (official)
Pitso 'Jingles' Mosimane
Rabbi Moripe
Sam 'Eewie' Kambule
Sonas Malope
Themba Ngwenya
Trott Moloto
Vincent Makroti
Walter Kutumela
William Zondi

Some of the notable Sundowns players during Natasha Tsichlas's era

Alex Bapela
Augustine Makalakalane
Bennet Masinga
Bennet Mnguni

Charles Motlohi
Daniel 'Mambush' Mudau
Eric 'Tambai' Ramasike
Gift Kampamba (Zambian)
Godfrey Sapula
Isaac Shai
Joel 'Fire' Masilela
John Tlale
Linda 'Mercedes Benz' Buthelezi
Lovers Mohlala
Matthew Booth

Muisi Ajao (Nigerian)
Philemon Masinga
Raphael 'Chukwu Train' Chukwu
Roger 'The General' Fetumba (Cameroonian)
Roger De Sa
Ronny Kananelo (Namibian)
Sizwe Motaung
Themba Mnguni
Zane Moosa

Acknowledgements

Writing the story of Zola Mahobe has been one of the most exciting experiences of my life. But it was no easy task, taking on a character as big as Zola Mahobe. 'This is the stuff movies are made of,' said many of those I told of my intentions to. Would I manage to do justice to it? I pray that I did. I wrote the first draft of the manuscript and submitted it to one of the major publishers, but they rejected it. I was dejected. Then I sent the manuscript to NB Publishers, where it found an angel of God waiting for it. This angel is Sonwabiso Ngcowa, my publishing editor, who, despite the manuscript being very rough and not so well written, believed in the story of Mahobe and decided to convince NB Publishers to offer me a publishing deal.

Then Sonwabiso brought on board Nikolaos Kirkinis to help with the manuscript development. It has been a great pleasure working with Niko, who not only pointed me in the right direction, but also helped with some of the interviews. He brought the book to life. I am also thankful to Mark Gleeson, former journalist for *The Star*, for his thoughts on the manuscript during its development. The cherry on top was Russel Brownlee, who came in to edit the manuscript. He was just what the book needed to bring a shine to it.

There are many other people I am thankful to for making this book possible. Among them I would like to single out Sipho Mahlaba, one of Mahobe's closest friends, who was willing to share his thoughts and experiences concerning Zola Mahobe.

I am also thankful to Mike Ntombela, former Sundowns player and captain of Sundowns during the Mahobe, Standard Bank, and Tsichlas eras. Bra Mike, as I call him, has since become a friend. I am also thankful to Johny 'Black Sunday' Masegela, a former Jomo Cosmos and Orlando Pirates striker, for sharing his experience of Mahobe.

My gratitude also goes to Zandile Thusi of the Standard Bank Knowledge Centre for providing documented information on Mahobe and Snowy's crimes from Standard Bank's side. Lastly, I would like to thank Natasha Tsichlas, former co-owner of Sundowns and a great friend of Mahobe's, for sharing her thoughts and stories about Mahobe and the team. Their contributions befitted the great man that Zola Mahobe was. Without these people, this book might never have seen the light of day.

About the author

Don Lepati is originally from Lesotho and became a permanent resident of South Africa in 1994. He is a former university lecturer and senior lecturer turned writer. He has lectured at the National University of Lesotho, the University of Zululand, the Medical University of Southern Africa (MEDUNSA), and the National School of Public Health. He has a BA (Economics & Statistics) degree from the National University of Lesotho and an MSc (Mathematics & Statistics) from Queen's University School of Graduate Studies and Research in Canada.